Also by Steve Chandler

100 Ways to Create Wealth (with Sam Beckford)

9 Lies That Are Holding Your Business Back (with Sam Beckford)

The Small Business Millionaire (with Sam Beckford)

Business Coaching (with Sam Beckford)

100 Ways to Motivate Yourself

17 Lies That Are Holding You Back

Reinventing Yourself

RelationShift (with Michael Bassoff)

The Joy of Selling

The Story of You

100 Ways to Motivate Others (with Scott Richardson)

The Hands-Off Manager (with Duane Black)

50 Ways to Create Great Relationships

Two Guys Read Moby-Dick (with Terrence Hill)

Two Guys Read the Obituaries (with Terrence Hill)

Ten Commitments
to Your
Success

by
Steve Chandler

Robert D. Reed Publishers • Bandon, OR

Robert D. Reed Publishers
P.O. Box 1992
Bandon, OR 97411
Phone: 541-347-9882 • Fax: -9883
E-mail: 4bobreed@msn.com
web site: www.rdrpublishers.com

Typesetter: **Barbara Kruger**
Cover Designer: **Grant Prescott**

ISBN 1-931741-50-6

Library of Congress Control Number 2004097950

Manufactured, typeset and printed in the United States of America

To Jessica, Stephanie, Mar and Bobby

Acknowledgments

Many thanks to George Pransky, whom Colin Wilson has rightfully identified as America's most visionary psychologist, from whose books and audio programs I have learned so much.

To Kathy, my wife and partner, who makes "commitment to your partner" the easiest commitment I have in life.

To Robert Reed, a publisher with a heart and a soul.

To Fred Knipe for sharing the acting, the songwriting, the comedy, the meditation and the ancient Chinese secret breathing techniques that lead to superhuman powers.

To Dr. Merlin F. Ludiker for having the courage to create a one-man play and the wisdom to see the unmanifest comedic field to which we are all connected.

To Tom Rompel for the distinction of commitment.

To Jack Cooper for the poetry, Terry Hill for the whale-watching and lifelong friendship, Sam Beckford for the breakthroughs in business coaching, Duane Black for showing me where success comes from, Tita and Pete for the Sundays in Tucson, Ral Donner for teaching us all that you don't know what you've got until you lose it, Blavdak Vinomori for the political genius that he demonstrates with every keystroke, John Hoke for the great concert, Scott Richardson for sharing his *ki* and his violin teacher, Steve Hardison for the baptism into action, Jeanne and Ed for the many respites from the journey, Bob Hazen for inviting me into the pool, Ron and Mary Hulnick for creating the school, Leonard Cohen for the begging-bowl, Bob Dylan for letting us know what happens when you are lost in the rain in Juarez, and all the graduate students at The University of Santa Monica for sharing their soul-centered leadership.

Contents

Introduction: How to organize your energy 1

Commitment Number One: To Spirit 4

All fear is the ego's fear of death 6

Can you be glad to be unhappy? 7

Why don't we all take up acting? 8

The real source of an actor's misery 12

A mantra for manifesting depression 12

Commitment Number Two: To Mind 14

Come down off the roller coaster 14

Onward, inward and upward 17

But where does loneliness come from? 20

I am bored with my life and my work 21

You create states with thought 22

Commitment Number Three: To Action 24

Find a way to get over it 26

You can't get to courage from here 28

Time is the stuff life is made of 28

Clear intentions inspire the right actions 31

Use the power of negative thinking 34

Tack up the quote that starts the mind 35

Commitment Number Four: To Wealth 37

Know your destination in advance 39

No difference? No money! 39

You get better at whatever you repeat 41

Exceptionality is the real problem 43

Difference-making at its very best 45

Wipe out poverty at home 46

Commitment Number Five: To Friends 47

Why is it unusual to like as well as love? 49

Commitment Number Six: To Commitment **51**
    Getting clear on what I'm committed to 52
    Commitment allows for backsliding. 53
    Commitment is a deep way of *being* 54
    Stop hoping that things will turn out 55
Commitment Number Seven: To Your Partner **58**
    Destroying the make-wrong machine. 61
    Would I rather be right than happy?. 62
    Release from the grip of the undertow 64
Commitment Number Eight: To Career **65**
    Stop trying to figure out *how to* do it. 66
    You don't have to make the right choice 67
    Leave your manager out of the equation 68
    When does a sale occur?. 69
    Use your email to build your career. 70
    A great career means taking responsibility. 71
    Create your own path to career success 72
    Success is getting *into* the box 73
Commitment Number Nine: To Body **75**
    Taking the emotion out of weight loss 77
    The stars on my pocket calendar 78
    It's time to learn to feed the dragon 80
Commitment Number Ten: To Your Music **84**
    I want to get all my boats to float. 85
    Losing the fear of not being good 87
Recommended Reading **89**
About the Author **90**

"What we seek as our highest goal
depends upon what we believe ourselves to be."

RAMANUJA

Introduction

How to organize your energy

"Great things are not done by impulse,
but by a series of small things brought together."
Vincent Van Gogh

One of my own dysfunctions in life had always been to focus on one or two of these ten commitments and let the others just fall apart.

If I'd get on a health kick, I'd spend too much time at the club and neglect other areas of my life. After they were neglected long enough, they would howl out for repair, so I'd turn my focus on them to the exclusion of my health.

It wasn't until recently that I realized that all ten would get better once I learned to keep all ten alive every day. It was called synergy, and I'd never understood synergy before.

The great visionary architect and scientist Buckminster Fuller defined synergy as "the behavior of whole systems, unpredicted by knowledge of the component parts."

Fuller uses the example of two metals combining to be stronger than the sum total of each metal. Why are they stronger? Because of the interaction of their molecules when they are put together.

Synergy for the ten commitments means the same thing. The molecules of each commitment interact and strengthen the others. When you're feeding all ten each day with care and attention, then the molecular structure of each interacts with the others and makes the whole more powerful than the sum of the parts.

Buckminster Fuller proved in his work that most people do not know it is possible to get more out of a system than you put into it. To get more than you pay for.

At first, when I was reading about Fuller's life I thought, "But that's architecture and design theory...does it really apply to a human life? Surely the same laws don't apply. This is flesh and blood and emotions, not metal."

But, that's the secret beauty of Buckminster Fuller's life. He applied these principles to his *own life*, too. And what a gift to us that he did. Because Fuller's life was not easy. Not until he applied the synergy.

In 1922, Buckminster Fuller's first child died in his arms of pneumonia just a month before her fourth birthday, after having survived both infantile paralysis and spinal meningitis. Fuller felt he was personally to blame for her death, which he thought could have been prevented if he had provided adequate housing and a properly designed environment. Imagine the pain of thinking that.

Then, in 1927, he lost a building company, which he had founded with his father-in-law, to bankruptcy. Couple that with personal bankruptcy the same year, and then add the birth of a new daughter. The pressure was unbearable. He stood on the edge of Lake Michigan and contemplated suicide.

The birth of his new daughter had pushed him to the edge of the water. He had to make a decision. It had to either be suicide or complete personal reinvention. There was no middle ground for him. His old chaotic way of life would only endanger his new child.

"I had really been through a great deal," said Fuller. "But I had gone into Harvard with high honors in physics. I had very rich boyhood experience with boats. In the Navy, I had looked into electronics, the chemistries and navigation. I had papers to command unlimited tonnage on the ocean. I could fly. But I had kept pushing things, trying them out. And it always seemed to come to a dead end. I decided I'd better call myself to account, with this new child to care for. Or get myself out of the way, because I was a mess."

A commitment is a silent decision inside

That's when Fuller made his commitment.

"At the age of 32 I decided to reorganize my effectiveness to recapture the capabilities we were born with," he said. "This is really where I started. I was not called an architect. I was not called anything. I was simply faced with the problem of organizing myself and really starting to use *me*. I had to educate myself in a great many ways to pursue such a course. But I found it's actually possible for an individual to make first moves, and that these will incite various others."

Fuller's enormous success thereafter was based on his many "first moves." He found that when he created a plan, and then made a series of first moves, he was creating and producing his life with action. Most people wait for the first moves to happen *to* them. They let the world around them make the first moves and then they respond, living a life of second moves, all in response to others.

Fuller also saw that the breakthrough would be to make a commitment to "reorganize" himself, all those individual parts of himself that had not yet been working in synergy, but rather pulling in all different directions. It took working in synergy, with all of his commitments firing at once, to recapture the capabilities he was born with.

Fuller wasn't the first person to become enlightened to the possibility of one's work, when done right, being a perfect model for a whole life done right. Ludwig van Beethoven once said, "He who understands my music will not be tormented by the ordinary difficulties of life."

When chaos escapes into a higher order there is synergy. This not only happens in science and physics, it happens in our own chaotic lives. Balancing these ten commitments will bring you a synergy you could not have imagined while you were busy fighting off the chaos.

The danger and the beauty

The danger involved in living a life of chaos is that spirit will never find a place to enter in. Happiness will be confused with pleasure, and anxiety will be confused with energy.

The beauty of a life organized around all ten commitments (including the vital commitment to commitment itself) is that one will experience life to the fullest. One will experience that paradox of a thoroughly exciting life of action with absolute peace at the center of it all.

Commitment Number One

To Spirit

"Must we light a candle
to see the sun?"
Albert Einstein

Spirit is like the wind. Because the wind can be a ruthless tornado or it can be light as the breeze. You know it's there. You just can't see it. You know it by the effect it has. You can feel it. It can level a town. It can lift a kite into the air. The wind can sail a boat around the world.

Spirit is like that. It can do that and more. You know it by the work it does although you can't touch it or hold it in your hand or put it in a safe deposit box…you can't save it or hoard it, and although most of the individual religions say, "We have the only real version of it," it's there for every living being.

Whatever spiritual practice and growth means to you, it is important. It can save your life. Do not neglect it. Commit to it. Then you'll know its power by the results it gives you. It will come into your life like the wind.

Or like a 12-step program of recovery from an addiction. You are amazed by the results. I went into one of those spiritual programs over 20 years ago and the spirit in that program saved my life. No drug or physician could have done that. No willpower or strength of character could have done that.

Some say this spiritual part of life is not really real. But how can something that saves one's life not be real? In fact, it's *more* than "real." It goes beyond everyday reality. It goes deeper. It reaches in there further.

I have had people ask me if my 12-step meetings weren't just some form of cult. Just people controlling people. These are people who have become upset when their own recovering family member gets "too far into" his or her spiritual program. I've had people ask me seriously if their family member might need some professional cult de-programming.

I remind those people that I am a person who has used a 12-step recovery program to get clean and sober and find a life, who has attended hundreds of meetings, met thousands of people, and I cannot find anything in my memory that would require de-programming. The meetings are so diverse, with so many colorful devil's advocates and iconoclasts in them, that they were anything but a cult. They were always more of an open inquiry into how to replace the false spirit with true spirit.

Addicts are spiritual seekers flying down the wrong road. They are in search of a shortcut to spirit. So addicts become trapped in illusory spirit, a fool's gold of uplifted feelings that mock the spirit and eventually become their own opposite. Soon, almost as a cosmic-sized joke, the addict must increase his addictive substance just to feel like a mediocre average human.

But join the 12 steps of spiritual recovery and something wonderful happens. False spirit is replaced. Real spirit blows into your life like a tornado.

The first step in most programs is realizing you have become powerless (helpless) over something. Be it drugs, booze, gambling, or whatever. People often tell me that this confession of powerlessness seems to contradict the message in my earlier books about the huge untapped power we have to create great lives.

But the "powerlessness" we have over what we are addicted to has no relationship to the powerlessness people lie to themselves about in other aspects of their lives: relationships, wealth, career, physical strength and vigor, spiritual joy, time management.

When a 12-step person accepts powerlessness he is accepting it in only one narrow (albeit potentially fatal) area. Alcohol (or cocaine or gambling or whatever) is one billionth of the available human life adventure. Of a billion things, it's the only thing we can't do.

Once addicted, an alcoholic is powerless over alcohol (or whatever drug)…in the sense that he is powerless to "control" the use in a non-addictive way since the *code is already in the brain* for addictive usage (whether it's a genetic code or repeated-usage code doesn't really matter). And that code is so strong it overrides willpower. So, yes, the 12-step programs are right.

"Powerlessness," in this instance, is self-honesty.

But I wanted, in those earlier books, to expose the fallacy of powerlessness in all other aspects of life. We have huge power that we hide from ourselves. In fact, in my own 12-step recovery I found a power to live creatively by rising above and beyond my addiction and simply saying "no" to its evil forces. Taking a strong stand.

The paradox of "powerless" in 12-step is that the total acceptance of being powerless over the drug opens you to the availability of a far greater power. The power to allow spirit to work through you.

"Somebody once put it this way: 'What stands in the way
is the way.' And you realize that when you no longer
internally resist the form that this moment takes."
Eckhart Tolle

All fear is the ego's fear of death

My daughter Margery, when she was very young, had a terrible anxiety about death and dying. So I would often say to her, just to ease the pressure a little, "You are not your body. You have a body, but you are not your body, so when your body finally does die out, how do you know that you die too? Where were you before you were born? Just as you don't save your hair when you get a hair cut and bury it and put a tombstone up to memorialize it, you really don't need to save the 'body' when you die. You are not the body. You have had a thousand bodies, as fast as cells get replaced. Why save the last and worst one? Why not save all of them? Why save any? Do you save your fingernails? Your hair should not be saved. It was with you for awhile, like your body. It served a purpose, like your body did. Your hair was there to help you look great. You had great hair. People confirmed that you did. You had a body, too. But notice that I said that you *had* a body. I didn't say that you *were* a body. Who is the *you* that *has* a body? Because you are not your body. You may never die. Your body does, but you might not. That's the exciting part of all this. Maybe I'll see you forever."

I was taking a risk throwing some images together seeing if I might not inspire Margie to a higher order of thinking. I wasn't trying to improve her thinking, nor was I even recommending self-improvement, just awareness. Awareness caused by breathing more deeply into a bigger picture than was there before. Because "inspiration" means literally to "breathe in."

Many people say that my books and talks are about self-improvement. But not quite. Because if I practice "self-improvement," who's doing the improving and who's being improved? If I have a better self who can direct the improvement of the lesser self, why bother improving that self? Why not just stay there and keep being that better self? But who is it that sees my better self in action when I say I'm improving myself? Once I can see and notice that stronger self in me, who's doing the witnessing? Couldn't this go on forever? Couldn't this be eternity? I used to neglect these questions, and I had the shallower more fearful life because of that neglect. Spirit sometimes calls in the form of these questions.

Can you be glad to be unhappy?

A friend wrote recently that he was living alone in San Francisco and that he was unhappy. I wanted to help him out a little but I had very little time *so I just told him he wasn't unhappy.*

I figured that might do it. You never know! There is an intriguing field of psychology called Brief Therapy. I once went to a psychologist in that field and it was great and powerful. Maybe that's what I was trying to do: "You aren't unhappy. There. Solved?"

"How insensitive!" That's what he said. "How do you know I'm not unhappy? I really am unhappy."

Again, pressed for time, I told him he just *thought* he was unhappy. I thought he might comprehend this dialogue I had just made up for him:

"How is your ex-husband?"

"I don't know. I try not to think about him."

"Is he happy?"

"He thinks he is."

So my point to my friend was that *you are not your mind*. You *have* a mind, but you are not your mind. Just as you have a body but are not your body. You have hair but you are not your hair. Who are you? Give up?

So when you write to me that you *are* "unhappy," at the being level, as if that is something that you exempt from the causative power of thought, or something that you want me to think has been caused by external events or other people, you only inspire me to go on like this because in all my imperfect coaching and workshops, my first passion and mission is to point out the causative power of thought. Why are children, by the way, exempt from the semi-permanent condition you call "unhappy"? Children are unhappy about 12 times a day and they are happy about 67 times a day. But it is not permanent. And they know it's not permanent, which is why they always very quickly move on from unhappiness to happiness. Adults try to make it permanent, like trying to nail Jell-o to the wall, which is exactly what suicidal Kurt Cobain was doing in the last apartment he lived in before committing suicide. Except that the Jell-o he ended up nailing to the wall was his own future.

"We are not troubled by things,
but by the opinion we have of things."
Epictetus

Why don't we all take up acting?

Once I took up acting to improve my skills in my seminars. I wanted to increase my ability to dramatize the points I was teaching and to be a fearless public speaker (something that had been somewhat of a problem for most of my life during which I was absolutely paralyzed with fear whenever I was in front of a group of people, or even reading aloud in a classroom).

And the acting classes were good for me, but not in the way I'd anticipated. Yes, I sort of increased my ability to be confident and expressive in my seminars, but that was small compared to the really big thing that happened in class.

The really big thing that happened was spiritual. For me it was. (And again, find your spirit anywhere, in your own chosen way or tradition, but find it and let it be, and then pass it on to any other broken-hearted people you know.)

Acting was about creating characters and actually becoming those newly-created personalities. (If you are not your body you are certainly not your personality.) When I acted in a local workshop version of *Dancing at Lughnasa* by the Irish playwright Brian Friel, something opened up in me that has been open ever since. It was never open before, but it has been open ever since.

Call it the creative me. Call it spirit. Somehow there was more of the creative me being used up in that whole rehearsal-to-performance process than I've experienced in any other activity. How could that be true, though? How could something so false be so true? I was making up a character! I was "faking" some weird character in an Irish play that was so unlike me that a choreographer had to come in to help show me how to move my body differently.

After that experience, and, believe me, I am a true amateur as an actor, I came away thinking that acting might be our highest professional accomplishment as humans! Why? Because, when we are successful, we are someone else.

My acting experience linked me more and more to what Deepak Chopra has been saying. What Alan Watts was saying, and, in a way, what Colin Wilson has been saying…our personalities, our identities are total fabrications. Especially to ourselves!

We are not totally separate from each other. Not really. It's all the same life energy dancing in the bloodstreams. When Jung spoke about our collective unconscious he didn't later say he was kidding about it.

I am not separate from you just as my index finger is not separate from my body. But when my index finger is activated? He thinks he is a separate fantastic thing pointing the way!

When we act, successfully, we *become* someone else. In Western culture, it is the accepted way of becoming a creator. Traditional scriptures say we were created in the image of our creator and our creator is nothing if not a creator of creators creating more creators.

Living in the image of your creator, you create humans. (A great novelist feeling the spirit does this, too.)

"We are building the spiritual equivalent of a muscle."
Nathaniel Branden

Deepak Chopra has always said to use meditation to become connected to spirit. To lose the artificial self known as the ego, one travels inward to the infinite. So one day I went with my friend Fred into the mountains of Arizona to meet someone who had been sanctioned by Chopra to teach his Primordial Sound Meditation (a version of the same Transcendental Meditation that Chopra had learned from his mentor the Maharishi.)

Chopra had said, too, in *Return of the Rishi*, that the only truly happy people he knows in life are meditators.

In meditation we leave the personality behind for the brief downward strokes when only the mantra is on our mind and we are sinking into the "unified field." Into the "unmanifest." We become peaceful when we are not living in our own personalities any more. Our own personalities are a creative fabrication designed to impress other human fabrications (which they never do because you can't impress a fabrication with a fabrication and you can't win over someone who is fictional to begin with).

When you can become everyone who ever lived you are happy. Kids often do that. They can easily become other people. They can even become mice. I was often Mighty Mouse as a child.

I rent movies like *Hoosiers* to watch Gene Hackman act. He could have retired many, many years ago. He could have opted to look out of windows on the Mediterranean with a thin cigar. No lines to learn. Many years ago. As businessmen do. (Retire. Like my father retired early. He "had to get out." Had to quit being his successful self. It's a real grind trying to maintain an exceptional character.) People long to retire who are maintaining a lie. The energy it takes to maintain the personality.

But actors don't retire. Why? Because they, too, are maintaining a lie, but they know it. In fact, it is their art form. They aren't pretending they're not pretending. They are just pretending, in the purest form. So why retire from something that liberating?

And, by the way, what do we even *mean* when we say something is "liberating?" Liberating from what? People are always saying that something wonderful is so *liberating*! What are you liberated from?

From the fabrication. From the fiction that is the personality. That's what we are liberated from.

When you take on a "character," you can soar. Why would anyone ever quit doing that? No one does, it seems. Newman. Redford. They all act until they die. Jack Lemmon. He was acting *while* dying (see *Tuesdays with Morrie*). Alec Guinness. Maggie Smith. And the incredible Jessica Tandy was 85 when she made *Nobody's Fool* with Paul Newman. She died that very year.

Are there a lot of other 85-year-old women working full time 10 hour days on location at their profession? Most women who are 40 are dying to get *out* of what they are doing. To quit and retire. They'd quit today if they could. That's why they think they'll stop off for a lottery ticket on the way home.

The actor sometimes tries to retire. Robert Redford said "I'll just be Robert Redford. I'll work for good causes. I'll direct!" And it is miserable after awhile being Redford. Just as we are miserable being who we are, it is miserable being Robert Redford. It was better being the Sundance Kid. That was better. Why? Because it was a fantasy? No, because he was using a fiction to liberate himself from another fiction. So Redford started acting again and again, long after he quit acting. He didn't need the money. He needed the liberation. It was exhilarating.

Maintaining that weird "real" fiction called Robert Redford is what is so hard. That's the hardest part about being an actor…going back to a character *not* created by William Goldman (the great writer who wrote the screenplay to *Butch Cassidy and the Sundance Kid*).

I believe that actors are miserable when they don't understand this dynamic and how spiritual it is. When they don't celebrate it. When they demean it and call it "compulsive workaholism." But none of them are miserable while they are "working" which is why they all work all the time. You never hear of an actor committing suicide *during* the filming or the run of a play. Why would they need to? They are already liberated, why do they need the liberation of suicide?

"If you don't find God
in the next person you meet,
it is a waste of time
looking for him further."
Mahatma Gandhi

The real source of an actor's misery

Many people have drawn the completely wrong and opposite conclusion about actors. They think actors are miserable because they have to be so phony in their characters all the time. Not true. The reason they are miserable (when they are, between projects, into their multiple marriages) is not because they pretend to be other people for a living. It's because they have to be "real" when the movie's over and they have no idea how to do it with a straight face. I think they are miserable because when the filming is over they think they have to really "be" themselves. I think they are fulfilled and experiencing spirit (the same thing) while working.

Some actors, on some level, understand that *they are their work*. They have accepted that they are not happy unless they are working. They are glad to have life be that way. So when they are not working, which is rare, they are not unhappy because they are serene in their anticipation of their next part. They feel the huge spiritual act involved in leaving your "self" completely behind in order to create that new character for the enjoyment of others.

A mantra for manifesting depression

The depressed person meditates on one mantra: "me, me, me, me, me, me." When people commit suicide they are killing the pain of trying to make that fabrication real.

Rather than obsessing about your unique personality and ego, why not pick something wonderful to create? Once you decide what that is, then *be who you need to be* to get it done.

Then you might want to step back a little, in prayer or meditation or a good long walk, and observe the patterns of thought that cloud up your brain and see how all those patterns obscure your spirit.

The body takes each thought and translates it into a feeling, which is a wonderful system if you are not swept away by cloudy, uncontrollable thoughts. If you can step back like this you are no longer swept away. Spirit moves into your life when you step back and observe. Spirit moves into the space between the observer and the observed thought.

The commitment you make to spirit, in whatever religious or non-religious form it takes, is absolutely vital to the other commitments being fully experienced and expressed. I have learned this the hard way by denying the reality of this most real aspect of human existence. As Chardin said, "We are not human beings having a spiritual experience, we are spiritual beings having a human experience." My commitment is to always know that, and to continuously grow upward into that ultimate "reality."

Commitment Number Two

To Mind

"The worst thing that can happen
to you is a thought."
Byron Katie

Happiness is our free-flowing state. Only toxic thoughts can contaminate that state. Happiness exists prior to thought. It's already in there for you. You don't have to go find it.

Why don't we always know this?

The *mind* is the problem.

Because you are reading this book with your mind, you are now using your mind. That's good. What's not good is when you are being used *by* your mind.

So a major commitment will be to use your mind. Not let it happen the other way around.

Most people get tangled up in the content of their minds, and soon they are identifying with that content. If the mind thinks, "I'm stressed, I'm overwhelmed," or "I'm depressed about this," then the mind has taken over your whole identity! It has staged a coup. The commitment that solves that problem is the commitment to *use* the mind. Your mind is a vehicle that exists to serve you.

If you want to use your mind rather than have it use you, you first must learn to become a version of being a mind whisperer. Like a horse whisperer. You must gently let it know who is in charge. Once you get in charge of your mind, you can ride it for pure enjoyment. And when you are threatened, you can ride it to higher ground and find the freedom you are longing for.

Come down off the roller coaster

Joey called to say he needed to talk. He was on a total "roller coaster" in his life, with all kinds of events taking him up and down, up and down. He wanted off the ride.

I recommended that he look at that roller coaster: Can you see it, Joey? If you can see it, you're not on it. The minute you step back, in breathing or meditation or insight, you are no longer identified with what's bothering you. Now you notice your thoughts. Don't you? If you are noticing your thoughts, you are no longer your thoughts. If you can see your train of thought, you are not on that train. True? If you can see a train pulling out of the subway station, you can't be on that train.

When you're on that roller coaster that Joey was on, don't try to *do* anything about it. Because going down and up is going to happen. Just don't worry so much about it, it's natural, and it's all caused by thought. Think one thing, up you go, think the opposite thing, down you go. Just notice how thought runs it. Just notice that. Don't try to change how thought runs it, just notice it. It will give you the necessary distance to navigate with if you remember to notice it. Most people don't notice, and therefore their thoughts are all taken too seriously. Thought becomes identity! But thought is just thought. Thoughts cross the mind like clouds cross the sky. And thoughts cause feeling just like clouds cause rain. Notice how it's your thoughts causing the up and down feelings. Notice that and you'll be fine. Once Joey noticed that, he was fine. He could get off the ride.

The first recognition of the mind's purpose is to see how it works best to solve your problems in life.

I used to think (and I only thought this for about thirty adult years!) that one must examine, introspect and understand all the problems that occupied the mind. That one must indulge and savor all of the mind's content. I believed that the deeper you went into that content, the better, because you had to "get to the bottom" of everything. Boy, was I wrong.

What I finally discovered along the way was that a more effective way to "solve" (or dissolve) a problem was to move my attention *off* the problem and *onto* the condition I would rather have, the condition that, if it existed, would make the problem no longer meaningful. It was the best use possible of the mind.

I finally broke this new insight into steps. You can do this right now with any problem you face. Step one is to *embrace* the problem and welcome it into your life. Let it have a seat and relax. Ask it many gentle questions so that you understand its entire nature. You are not afraid of it. You are learning to understand it. (We only fear what we don't understand.) You welcome it.

Sometimes the problem is another person. But again, you welcome it. That person exists to take you to a higher level of spiritual growth, no matter how frightening that person may be.

"My enemy is my best teacher," said the Dalai Lama.

Step two is to ask yourself whether a certain condition, a certain goal reached, would make the problem disappear (go away happy). If the answer is yes, then you dismiss the problem (different than denying or repressing it) from your mind, give the problem a final hug and ask the new potential condition to come in and take a seat.

Now I realize why that process works: when I worry and obsess about a problem, I go down into a bad mood: discouraged, gloomy, and all of a sudden very tired. *That* mood allows for no creativity, inspiration, enthusiasm, or intuition. In other words, that mood leads to dysfunctional, unresourceful thinking and it also makes the problem look huge (as I look up at it from way down there; problems have scary undersides).

In an expansive mood, as I float upward, my problem not only looks smaller, but I can see the condition I want, I can see some new options for how to get the good condition.

Example: a debt I owe is a problem…the more I think about it the less I can do about it. Why? I'm listless. I'm world-weary. I'm shut down with discouragement. Fear creeps in. What does my creditor *think* of me?

But sleep (or contemplative prayer or meditation or the deepest of breathing or a long walk) allows my mind to die and be born all over. It's a re-booting of the mind. Soon my whole being wakes up not thinking about the problem, but rather thinking about some new and good money-making opportunity. I seize one. I go do it. I haven't thought about the "problem" once, but once the new money-making idea is fully executed, the problem is dissolved! The new project has brought in enough money to wipe out that debt and then some.

Malcolm X went around screaming that racism was a problem that must be eliminated. Martin Luther King sized up the very real problem of racism, but then elevated his spirit up to the condition he wanted instead. King then went to the world and said "I have a dream." His poetic and powerful vision drew followers. It changed the world.

Who was more effective? Of the two men. Who made a bigger difference? Which one has a holiday?

Bringing something into existence turns out to be easier in the long run than eliminating something from existence. This is because the one activity is creative (and therefore uses the highest mind, the maximum whole-brain thinking) and the other is destructive and therefore uses only the lower animal brain.

"The natural inclination of a child is to take pleasure in the use of the mind no less than of the body. The child's primary business is learning. It is also the primary entertainment. To retain that orientation into adulthood, so that consciousness is not a burden but a joy, is the mark of the successfully developed human being."

Nathaniel Branden

Onward, inward and upward

There was a certain point where my life shifted ever so slightly and that was the point at which I finally understood something about the workings of the mind. Ever since that time, I've made my living showing the insights I got to others in hopes that they, too, might move onward (and inward) with this new understanding. It was subtle, this insight, but all-important. It was a final understanding of the role of thought.

Because in the past, I'd never fully understood the role of thought. I'd always assumed that the brain worked from the outside in, like a stimulus-response machine. Just waiting all day for stimulus. *What will happen to me?*

Here's an example of what I never saw before: If I am a little boy and I am sent to my room, and I listen through the door and I overhear my father say, "I never wanted him here. I've said from the start we need to get rid of him." I immediately might think he's talking about *me*, and I might be devastated for life. But what I didn't know was that my father was talking on the phone to an old buddy about their favorite team's football coach. ("I never wanted him here. We need to get rid of him.") I only thought (THOUGHT) he was talking about me. So my thought did me in. My dad didn't do me in, my thought did.

The breakthrough in this is that all of us live in separate realities created by thought. To change your reality, you can change your thinking.

The human brain is a biocomputer that few of us know how to use. But when you get this new understanding of the role of thought, life tends to get better.

Often, when I communicate the example of the boy and his father in one of my workshops, I get floods of letters and emails afterward. That's how I know that this insight is making a difference. Here's an email I got:

> Ever since you spoke at our 'Mandatory Meeting,' I have been so excited about the information you gave me! When I got home I shared what I learned with my husband and he was really excited too. (I believe it was because I was being a whiny victim the night before! ;) What a great gift you have to share with others, I am very glad I had the opportunity to listen to you. I love learning about new ways to improve my life and assist my children in learning better ways to utilize their lives here.

When people increase their effectiveness and their enjoyment of life, it comes from an increase in understanding…not from attitude, character, personality, willpower, inner strength, or any of the other mysterious imponderables that people use to shame themselves and others with. It comes from simple understanding.

It has nothing to do with IQ, really. You can find a third world person with the highest IQ in his country and he won't be able to use the Google search engine until he gets an understanding of it…instead, he'll be in a long line at the library and may even take months to get the information he wants while a low IQ person who understands Google could have gotten it for him in twenty seconds.

Google is your mind.

Because intelligence is vastly overrated as to how far it can take you…it might be fun to have a lot of it…it was fun for me to score relatively high on an IQ test long ago but it didn't save me at all from being suicidal about my ineffectiveness at making the very basic things in life work for me.

At one period in my life I went into therapy as a way to see if I could solve my problems. And it occurs to me now, that although I received huge unintended benefits from being in therapy, the therapy itself was not complete, because it was leaving something important out. It was trying to understand each individual's personal patterns of dysfunctional psychology, and then label those patterns, and then "work on" them. But it never fully "worked" for me because there was no accompanying attempt to understand the basic principle of thought.

When thought enters the body, a feeling is the result. And the process is that predictable.

People think their way into trouble, and then study the trouble. They think their way into anger or depression, and then they study the depression and anger. Can you see the fallacy there? The thinking itself is never studied.

Let's look again at the example of the boy sent to his room overhearing his father say "I never wanted him" in the other room. That boy/man might later go into therapy and study his own feelings of abandonment, his lack of trust, his sense that his parents favored his younger brother, etc. And every time those subjects came up he would be encouraged to cry and scream and feel those feelings even deeper.

This is like saying if you have a broken arm you have to come in and break it even more.

What that boy/man does not understand is that *thought* causes everything he feels. Not his father. After all, he only *thought* his father didn't want him. But even if his father looked him in the eye and said he didn't want him right to his face it would only be the *thought* that his father didn't want him that depressed him.

Feelings are good to feel deeply and release, but the therapy I was in skipped the role of thought. If you are studying the weather, you don't just study the rain. You study the cloud systems, too. For they have caused the rain.

By bypassing the role of thought we prematurely seek to understand each "unique" individual human instead of starting out by understanding all humans.

The past cannot affect you in any way if you are not thinking about it. Notice, when you step back, that you are not your thought. You are whatever is witnessing your thought. Who is it that is witnessing your thought?

"Closer is he than breathing, nearer than hands and feet," said Alfred Lord Tennyson. For Tennyson, "he" was simply the witness of the thinker of the thoughts.

But where does loneliness come from?

My daughter Stephanie was troubled the other day about something occurring at her job. She called to ask, "Dad, where do you think loneliness comes from? I know that it is an emotion that is caused by the thought process. But how is it that people can be surrounded by others and still feel loneliness? I'm just curious on your thoughts on the subject. What would your advice be if someone told you that they were lonely to the point where they could physically feel it?"

I made a try to help her see something. Not because I always know ultimate truth, but because it just might help. I said that it was my opinion that loneliness comes from thought. Thoughts about being so lonely. You can't feel lonely without thinking you are lonely. The best known cure is to get out of your self-obsession and drop the hobby of thinking so much about yourself and *help* somebody. You can't be lonely or depressed while helping someone else. It's impossible for the mind to hold those two activities simultaneously.

You can help by doing a good job for everyone around you and your customers at work, by helping everybody you see. You can help by listening to people. By appreciating them. You can help by helping. I once heard a very wise person named Zig Ziglar give a speech in which he said, "You can get anything you want in life if you help enough other people get what they want."

Stephanie wasn't satisfied with my wise observations. She pressed on and asked, "But how is it that people can be surrounded by others and still feel loneliness?"

"Because they are still *self*-obsessed, maybe?" I offered. "They are not interested in the people they are surrounded by. Tell them to get interested, listen and help. You can help others just by listening. Then give them ideas and other things, connections to people, that will really help them. You can't be lonely while doing that. Impossible. And if you don't feel interested in them, fake it until you do. You will. You can get interested in anything. Stay with it."

I am bored with my life and my work

I was mildly surprised during lunch with a friend whom I had admired when he said as we were leaving that he had become "bored" with his life and work. I was too tired to say anything, so I just took it in. I knew he had wanted some kind of discussion about it, but now that lunch was over, it was too late to get into it. We had run out of time. Besides, the proper setting would be a conference room with a white board so I could show him some things. Later I did. Or tried to.

So here it is in a nutshell: a person cannot "be bored." Just as a person cannot "be angry" or "be depressed" or "be scared."

That's not how the mind works. A thought can't become your entire being and identity. (It can just feel like it has.) It's a very common human superstition (irrational fear based on myth) that if we are feeling something or thinking something we are "being" that.

Ancient cave dwellers thought the thunder would kill their small animals. Because it once happened that thunder accompanied a disease that killed a goat they forever linked thunder to the death of animals. They saw cause and effect where there was none. So it became a superstition (the myth soon grew that there was a Thunder God who got angry at various forms of human behavior).

We do the same thing in this society, we humans do, when we fail to notice thought. Something happens. Then we think about it, then we feel something. A memory comes up, then we think about the memory, then we feel something. Life happens. Then we think about it. Then we feel something. We think the feelings come from those events we're thinking about. But that's a mistaken misperception. The feelings come from the thoughts. All events are essentially neutral. Until thought begins. Until the spin begins.

When I feel something unpleasant (like boredom), it is my body's signal to me that my thought is contaminated and I am no longer free-flowing. In fact, that's *why* I feel the bad feeling…my body is trying to tell me to shift my thinking back to its natural resourceful, whole-brain state. (Or, even better, to drop thinking altogether for awhile.)

It's just like when I get a splinter in my foot and it feels so painful I can't walk on that foot, my body is giving me a gift of that feeling so that I can remove the splinter…remove the contamination from the free-flowing body.

You create states with thought

If I am bored, that's just a feeling I have. One cannot "be" bored. The brain doesn't permit outside circumstances to cause direct states of being. The brain, instead, allows you to create your own state of being through thought. Your state of mind cannot be caused by events . The events that happen to you in your life are essentially meaningless…they feel "real," just as "real" as that mountain you see, but that mountain can't "cause" you to feel anything or to think anything.

Your internal biology drives your thought into your consciousness. When that thought is a contaminated one, you know it because you feel something unpleasant: anger, fear, boredom, burn-out, annoyance.

If you slow down and take your thoughts back to neutral, or your mind into the state the Samurai warriors called "no mind," then you can create your own state of being. The being you want for the situation at hand.

The danger of not keeping this commitment to understanding and using your mind (instead of it using you) is that you'll always be confusing reality with the content of your mind. Also, you will not have any way to step back from your thoughts and just be. All the other commitments will be weakened by this fundamental misuse of the human mind.

The beauty of this commitment is that it puts you in the proper relationship with your mind. Your mind becomes a sparkling tool to be used and then set down when not needed or wanted.

Let's end this chapter with my two favorite quotes about the human mind. You might wonder about these quotes. You might even think they are not really about the mind. But notice, if you do think that, what you're thinking is just a thought:

> "It is well known that all ogres live in Ceylon, and that all their beings are contained in a single lemon. A blind man slices the lemon, and all the ogres die."
>
> **Jorge Luis Borges**

> "It's going to happen very soon. The great event which will end the horror. Which will end the sorrow. Next Tuesday, when the sun goes down, I will play the Moonlight Sonata backwards. This will reverse the effects of the world's mad plunge into suffering, for the last 200 million years. What a lovely night that would be. What a sigh of relief, as the senile robins become bright red again, and the retired nightingales pick up their dusty tails, and assert the majesty of creation!"
>
> **Leonard Cohen**

Commitment Number Three

To Action

"Courage is not the absence of fear, but rather the judgment
that something else is more important than fear."
Ambrose Redmoon

Why do we want courage anyway? Maybe it's because we think
that with enough courage, we will take action. We'll take the action
we need to take. To change the things we can change.

During my recovery from addiction many years ago I used to
worry about the "Serenity Prayer." We all said it at the start of our
12-step meetings. The prayer asked that we be granted the serenity
to accept the things we could not change. I was worried that it
might become like a spiritual tranquilizer to me: Accept. Accept.
Accept. Accept the things I cannot change.

I now see the wisdom of this acceptance. Only after accepting
what can't be changed can we move on and get into action on the
things we *can* change. But back then? I was obsessed with my lack
of courage. With my addiction to non-action.

So I wanted to focus on the second part of the prayer, the part
that asks that I be granted "the courage to change the things I can."
God grant me that courage! I thought I had a big problem because I
used to think the courage always had to come first. You applied for
a grant and you waited for your grant to come through. If you did
not receive the grant, you could not change the things you needed to
change because you had not been granted the courage to do so.

You were stuck with that weak personality of yours. It was a
personality that contained no courage.

But my understanding was off. By a lot. I had failed to see
something that, once I saw it, would change my life forever. It isn't

your personality that contains the courage. It's the *action* you take that generates the quality we call courage. Action generates courage, personality doesn't.

For example, if you save someone from a burning building it is not likely that you would say, "My personality ran in and saved the child. Boy, am I ever happy I have the personality that I have. And the child is happy too. Because of my personality, one that features courage, that child lives today!"

That would not be what you would say. Well, why not? Everything else in life is because of your personality, isn't it? All your failures and frustrations? All your bad fortune?

That's the culture's belief. And so it's not surprising that it's your belief. But when you saved the child you were just in action. It was the action that saved the child, and you know it. It wasn't some quality that previously existed in you.

I was recently given the opportunity to re-write and re-edit my book *Reinventing Yourself.* (It was appropriate that the publisher allowed me to reinvent a book on reinventing.) There was one essential change I wanted to make (and did) throughout the newly edited book. Originally the book gave the reader the impression that life's object was to reinvent yourself from one personality to another, from a weak personality to a strong one. Even the subtitle promised that the reader would learn to *Become the Person You've Always Wanted to Be.*

But that kind of reinvention was slightly off-target. In that form of reinvention you run the risk of trading one personality for another. But I have now discovered that the only reinvention that's worth anything is the reinvention from something to nothing, the reinvention from a personality (some thing) to pure action (no thing, just action), the reinvention you do when you change from being a noun to being a verb.

The contemporary poet Jack Cooper sent me this intriguing note after I'd helped him find the motivation to complete a writing project: "Your persistence is inspiring. I recall my older son, Jesse, asking my dad, a star basketball player in his day (he actually "invented" the jump shot, if you can believe it), how he was able to jump so high. At six feet tall he could stuff the ball. My father told him that every day he would set out to jump a quarter of an inch higher on the net until he was finally able to touch the rim, then grab the rim, then put his whole forearm inside the basket. It wasn't a question I ever asked because I got sick of hearing about basketball as a young man. Who would've thought he could just as well have been talking about poetry?"

Find a way to get over it

Are you afraid? Do you have a fear? The trick is really to just get over it.

And I don't mean "get over it" as in "put it behind you" or "let it be history" I mean "get over it" like *rise up so high that it's under you now. Get over and above it.*

Rise up so high on your vibratory scale of feelings that you can come from a higher place. When you do that, your fear is still there, but it's way down there. You can sink down and get into it if you want to, but why bother? From on high you can just *do* the thing you're afraid of doing. Vibration and action go together.

No one has more courage than you do. It might *look* like people have more courage than you, but they don't. When you see a "brave" act by someone else, such as a person jumping off a cliff into water, or running a 100-mile ultra-marathon or speaking in front of 1,000 people, you are probably not seeing courage at all, but rather the result of practice. It looks like courage, but it's just practice. Don't confuse courage with practice. I did that for years and it kept me from doing so much I could have been doing. I see so many people today confused about this, too. They think they don't have courage, and they miss the whole point of courage. They have not practiced. And that's all that's missing.

Fear only succeeds in stopping us when we don't have a sufficient goal or crisis in front of the fear. One of the best ways to overcome a fear is to place it down there in the road between you and something you really want.

If you really want to save your little dog from the burning building, and you can hear her barking inside, you are likely to set aside your fear of the fire and *push through* the flames to get to her and bring her out. Once you get her out you are exhilarated, not just from having saved her, but also from having done something you never would have thought you could do. You are always larger and stronger than your fear, but you don't know it.

"The future enters into us, in order to transform itself in us,
long before it happens."
Rainer Maria Rilke

For most of my life I feared speaking in front of people. I was larger and stronger than that fear, but I didn't know it. If the old me could see me today he would be absolutely astonished. He would see someone who enjoys and looks forward to getting connected to a crowd of people, the larger the crowd the better. But it wasn't courage that reinvented me, it was practice.

Courage is often expressed by acting so quickly that the fear doesn't have time to sink in—if I am afraid to throw my warm body into the icy waters off the shore, I can best do it by jumping in before I think too much about jumping in. This is called taking your fear by surprise—you kind of sneak up on it and you surprise it with an unexpected action.

Say the boss asks for a volunteer to emcee the company talent show and even though you had a fear of speaking in front of people, you hear yourself saying "I'll do it!" even before you've thought it through.

That example also illustrates another way to outsmart fear: commit to do something you're afraid to do—promise someone else you'll do it, someone you wouldn't break a promise to.

When I joined the army and we were signing up for the final induction, I stepped aside for a moment and told myself I couldn't do it. I just couldn't sign the final papers and become a soldier for four years—especially since this was the Viet Nam era and you never knew for sure what would happen. As I started to walk away I remembered that my friend Fred was in the same building somewhere signing his final papers. We had signed up together and agreed to go in together. If I had walked away I would have broken that promise to him—I wouldn't have been able to live with myself after that. So I walked back to the last table, signed the last papers, walked down the hall and got on the bus that would take me away for four years. I was glad I did that.

Sometimes I have used food to cover up fear—if the fear is too uncomfortable I would load up the system on food! It blurs the consciousness just enough. So I'd pull up to the electronic menu and I'd say, "Give me three cheeseburgers, a vanilla shake and some chili fries and a cookie. A large cookie. A very large cookie! Oh please, make it a big cookie."

How sad. How sad to misunderstand fear this way and run and run and run.

You can't get to courage from here

When it comes to courage, the one thing to remember is that courage isn't some difficult place to get to. Nor is it a "characteristic" locked in somewhere on my DNA spiral. You don't climb arduously upward toward it. There is not straining, striving and forcing your way up to the promised pinnacle of courage. That's not where courage is. Courage already exists in an unused rhythm inside you. It is engaged and activated by a form of spinning outward and outward, like a beautiful, lighthearted dance. We call this dance practice.

If you think courage is outside of you and you must strive and climb to get to it you will never have it. You can't get there from here. Because "there" is *already* "here." The dance is in you. And soon you dance just to dance. Why else do you dance? To get someplace? Do you dance to get from one place on the floor to another?

So the easy steps to courage don't ascend. They shuffle. And they slide, and they spin and tap and click, glide and hop around the floor. They are dance steps. The easy steps are like the Mambo. Or the Funky Chicken. Or the Mashed Potato. Or The Stroll. Or the waltz, or the Soupy Shuffle. The steps are easy. Although the practice at the beginning can feel hard.

Time is the stuff life is made of

If I want to start living a life of action, it's important that I learn to honor time. That I learn to choose what to do with my small allotments of linear time.

I have attended a great many time management seminars, and have read many more books on the subject. My home office library alone (I just went and checked) has 12 books on managing time! However, I've yet to see or read anything better than the system proposed by St. Francis of Assisi many, many years ago. St. Francis said, "Start by doing what's necessary, then what's possible, and suddenly you are doing the impossible."

But, St. Francis! That can be a hard system to follow! Because it is easier to live a distracted life of chaos than to really get my necessary things done. A self-dramatized life in which I feel swamped like a victim. That is the easiest way to live. (Not easy in a positive sense, but "easy" in a passive, lonely, negative sense.) That is the easiest way for humans in our society to be: to be swamped, to be overwhelmed, to be overworked, to feel the drama of being a victim. Especially those of us who have our own businesses, because we really could work 24 hours a day. We would have plenty to do. If we could find a way to stay alert and awake for 24 hours, we could work 24 hours. We wouldn't run out of things to do. But that's the problem. It is being overwhelmed by things, it's being unwilling to have a plan and then work it. Instead we work everybody else's plan. Our creditors' plan, our spouse's plan, our customers' plan, our anxiety's plan.

This sense of dramatic overwhelm is the biggest problem people have today. It leads to bizarre phantom concepts like "multitasking."

And so the way to focused *action* lies in becoming your own mentor. Developing and nurturing that inner counselor so that your higher self makes all the decisions throughout the day on what you're going to do with your time. That's your true commitment to action.

Because without a plan, you run your day based on your fears. You check in each morning with your sense of dread. What do I dread? What do I hope won't happen?

These fears are something that we multiply in our mind, and we multiply them so that every fear soon becomes multiplied by a factor of about 100. The fear-times-100 then becomes much worse than doing the actual thing would be, and then *by not doing it* it grows and grows. And then finally, if for some reason we just *have* to do it, we're really exhilarated and we almost feel giddy because, "My gosh, it really wasn't so bad after all!"

There's only one way around that. And that is to find a way to walk toward that fear and deal with it in a way that isn't frightening. Now, if people will take time, they will be able to come up with a way, a routine, a structure, to deal with any fear they have in grown-up life. A way that does not scare them. But they don't take the time to figure this out because they're too afraid to even look at the fear.

Avoidance feeds the fear. Fear gets its sustenance and nutrients from avoidance. Understanding this, Emerson said, "The greatest part of courage is having done it before."

I can overcome fears if I allow myself to understand how powerful my mind really is. Because if I relax my mind and let it float up into its most creative state, I can see that there are ways to *do* things without actually "doing" them.

For example, I used to have a profound fear of public speaking and, like most people with a fear, I thought 'I can't do that. That's something I can't do.' But when I realized that I *had* to do it to make my profession complete, I then developed ways to trick myself into not being afraid, to build up to it, to do a little bit at a time, to just do inch by inch. I'd practice in front of the mirror, then in front of my family, then in front of a small group. And you can do that inching-up system with any fear. Anybody can.

If I am afraid of confronting a co-worker, I can confront him without really confronting him. I can talk to him in my car on the way to work until it feels more natural and strong to do so. Or I can just sit with him for awhile first and allow him to pour his heart and soul out to me. Soon we're on a level of connection and relaxation where the "confrontation" becomes easy. Just an exchange of information.

If I am afraid of jumping out of an airplane, I can sneak up on it by jumping off a chair, then jumping off a roof, then jumping a few times off a tower, so that I'm doing it but not yet really doing it.

When I feared public speaking I practiced my talk to one person, then to three people, then to a team meeting, then to the mirror 20 times, so I was doing it without doing it. If I'm afraid of dogs I can buy a puppy, which is not really a dog yet, and raise the puppy.

With fear, I need to outsmart the fear because fear is big but stupid. And fear gets embarrassed easily. When it has to live inside the infinite energy field of the human spirit, fear gets very embarrassed and runs away.

Many of my clients who think they have astonishing, horrible fears, are often surprised to see that there are ways to approach their fears by moving toward them, not running away from them. They find ways to completely embarrass the fear and make the fear look stupid.

You have to practice it, and sometimes someone has to be there to help show you how capable you really are of doing that thing that you're afraid to do.

Many famous sports coaches have told their teams, "It's not the will to win that matters, it's the will to prepare to win."

But if I am lost in my chaos, and I am swamped, and I am problem-solving and firefighting, and that's how I'm running my life, then I'm not preparing to win. What I'm doing is meeting and fending off immediate emotional needs, and that is a very ineffective way to grow a career committed to action. The way to grow that career is to *prepare* to win. So if I want to win new customers or new clients or new members or anything that will grow my career, then what I need to do is to block out time for preparation, instead of just winging it and running around. All that winging that I do is based on short-term gratification. Avoidance of pain instead of laying the groundwork for happiness.

But if I take a long-term approach, I might ask myself, "What if I really *had* to get X amount of new customers in the next three months, how would I approach it?" The answer is that I would take my time. I would prepare, I'd be strategic. I'd be like a chess master. Like the great chess master Kasparov whose motto was, "Think seven moves ahead." I wouldn't be this emotional person winging it, overwhelmed, melting down, and anxiety-ridden every day. That's absolutely not necessary as a way to live.

Clear intentions inspire the right actions

The right goals inspire the right action. When I do a goal achievement seminar, I work with groups such as sales people and people who are growing their businesses, and the very first step in the seminar is to realize once and for all that the *process* goal and the *outcome* goal are two different things. And once you get the difference clear in your mind you can use them both effectively to determine your day of actions.

For example, if my *outcome* goal is to have ten new clients every month, then that's the outcome that I want. From there, I can use *process* goals to produce my outcome. Most people don't do this. All their goal-setting is outcome-based so their minds remain anxiously focused on what they don't have. They live in the future, which is the root of all anxiety. They can't relax into the process of now. They try to push the river upstream instead of just going beautifully along with the river, stroking along with it and feeling the cold rush of the water on their skin making them really come alive in the moment.

A *process* goal is any goal that I can guarantee reaching. For example, let's say I set a process goal to call four prospects before I go to lunch. And so I put my notebook down by the telephone and I put four circles on the page and I say to myself, "Before I go to lunch today, I'm going to call four client prospects on the phone. And as I call each one I'll put an X in the circle and when all the circles are filled I'll go to lunch." That's a process goal.

Now say the person next to me also has the job of getting clients like I do. If he's like most people he will say to himself, "Well, I'd better call some people; that's probably the right thing to do." So he'll pick up the phone to make some calls. But then a friend of his comes by his desk and says, "Let's go to lunch." And he hesitates and finally says, "Oh, okay. People have to eat." And then he gets up and goes to lunch. A few minutes later another person will come by to me, and say "Let's go to lunch," and I will say, because I have a process goal in place, "I've got two more calls I have to make. When I make those calls I'll join you. Where are you going to be?"

Most people would *never* say, "calls I *have* to make," if they had only told themselves to make calls. They would only say "I have a call I have to make" if some outside person had said "You have to call them," or "You have to call me." And that's the beauty of the process goal. It changes your life from outside impetus to inside impetus. Rather than letting the outside world's expectations dictate your actions, you let your own goals dictate your actions.

That's what most people *don't* do with their time. They don't set up their own system for their own process goals. They let outside forces dictate what they think is necessary. They forget their own power and only recognize the power of others.

"Shallow people believe in luck,
wise and strong people believe in cause and effect."
Ralph Waldo Emerson

If I want to look like a trim gymnast by the time of my high school reunion, that's an *outcome* goal and I put a picture of a gymnast on my wall. Now my *process* goal would be to do 50 push-ups every morning. I know I can do 50 push-ups every morning, and I can check it off on my refrigerator pad. The great thing about process goals is that you can always do them, and they give you great satisfaction when you check them off.

Or, for another example, let's say my outcome goal is to get 10 new clients a month and so I set a process goal of doing 20 hours a week of client cultivation, and I check it off, and I log in and I log out and I keep track down to the minute to make sure I put in those 20 hours, because I always want to make sure that I do my process goal. Now after a couple of months, maybe I'm getting eight clients a month instead of 10. So now I change my process goal to 24 hours a week of cultivation, and then I look at my outcomes after that. You can keep altering your process until the outcome is hit.

If you don't put the process goals in, the outcome goals are just a matter of fortune, luck, and they create a tremendous anxiety about your life.

The reason my explicit process goals are important is that I don't want to assume that I'm always going to be in the same state of mind, and that I'm always going to be inspired, and even that I'm always going to *remember what I'm up to!* I don't want to assume that. So I want to have those process goals charted and tracked so that I do them no matter what thinking state I'm in.

And then I also want advertise back to myself what it is that I'm up to. What's my outcome goal? What am I here to achieve? And so I use all kinds of little things. I put sayings and slogans up where I can see them. I post my goals by my computer, because this human mind of mine is so distractible I want to ambush it with purpose. (It is estimated that humans have 40,000 thoughts a day, and only a very few of those are about their definite major purpose in their day.)

I want to keep bringing myself back on course, so I want to advertise to myself. I want to conspire with myself to keep myself in action.

If I've read a really wonderful book that I was inspired to action by, I don't want to just put that book away and say, "Boy, I hope I get that feeling again someday with some other book." That makes me a victim of fate and fortune. I want to be an owner of action. I want to produce my fate. So instead I open the book again and put it by my computer. Each day I will re-read one page from that book. Because that puts me back in charge of inspiring my own action.

Use the power of negative thinking

Action isn't always about positive thinking, either. Sometimes being negative is a good way to start.

Because you always have clarity on *what you don't want*. When an alcoholic quits drinking, there's a point at which he draws a line in the sand and says, "Okay, no more. That's it. No more of that way of life. I will not go there." That's a *stand*. That's why, in some ways, the negative can be a great place to start when creating an action plan. It gives you the commitment: Given that you don't ever want to be a drunk again, what are the action steps you can take to absolutely insure that it doesn't happen again? (It turns out there are twelve.)

If I'm trying to get people to write what their goals are and to make a list of what they want to achieve in the next year, quite often that's difficult. Quite often people get stuck and say, "Well, I just don't know what's important to me, I don't know what I really want."

So what I'll say is, "All right, then, I understand that. So why don't you write down what you absolutely *don't* want. What do you hope doesn't happen?" Because all people are really clear on that. They say, "Well, I don't want to go into debt, I don't want to go out of business." And I say, 'Okay, great, keep writing.' When they put down the things that they *don't* want, we convert those into goals: "Okay, you don't want to go into debt. So what you want to be is profitable, right? You want to have ongoing profit, that guarantees you don't go into debt, and so you want to *operate* at a profit. Good, so write that down."

People can take the negative and flip it around and then really know what they want.

Tack up the quote that starts the mind

I love to post quotes up to remind me what commitment to action is really all about. The quotes change a lot, because a lot of time quotations and phrases come to me at a new level of growth and they mean something they never meant before. If you're asking me today what quote means the most, I think the one quote that I would want live by and would want all my clients and everybody I train to have is a quote that says: "Only the disciplined are free."

Only the disciplined are free. Because there is no freedom in being undisciplined at the mercy of market, weather, employee complaints. There's no freedom in that. There is total bondage and chaos. The more disciplined I am with my actions, and with my precious time, the more disciplined I am in who I choose to communicate with and where I choose to place those 40,000 thoughts each day. The more disciplined I become, the more free I am to have the life I want. If I conduct myself in a disciplined and organized way, I have much more free time.

Discipline has gotten a bad name. People use it to mean punishment. And I don't mean it that way. Discipline comes from the word "disciple." So it feels better when it means "being your own disciple." Following your own best advice.

Becoming more disciplined about which actions to take has real-life, day-to-day applications and immediate benefits. (Otherwise, why grow it and develop it?) In Eknath Easwaran's wonderful book, *Conquest of Mind*, he writes, "The Buddha, the most practical of teachers, defined the wise man or woman in a thoroughly practical way: 'One who will gladly give up a smaller pleasure to gain a greater joy.' "

A commitment to action is fundamental to a happy life.

I like to center my commitment to action on what I call the "quit switch" at the center of my whole energy system. The action commitment is a commitment to practice *not* throwing that quit switch in the face of fears and obstacles.

The danger of not keeping my commitment to action lies in losing that muscle. Every time I choose no action when action is appropriate, that muscle gets weaker. I need my commitment to action because it is what pumps energy and breakthroughs into all the other commitments.

Commitment Number Four

To Wealth

"Someday I want to be rich. Some people get so rich they lose all
respect for humanity. That's how rich I want to be."
Rita Rudner

Wealth is a matter of having enough. For you. However you
define it. So it has a strong connection to the skill of knowing and
then getting what you want.

And the first rule of getting what you want is this: *You'll get
what you want faster when you know what it is.*

Lack of intention is a disorder. A person on the street walking
one way, then another, then in circles, suffers from a deficit of
intention.

We are driven by our intentions. Yet we act as if we don't know
that. We act as if we are driven by circumstances and obstacles that
pop up unexpectedly.

For wealth to occur in our lives, we need to gather a new
respect for intention. We need to commit to it.

By not being clear about our intentions, we fall into disorder.
We are swamped and overwhelmed by problems. We have all kinds
of people making all kinds of demands on our time.

Because if we are caught up in this swirl of activities, not
even knowing where we are going, we won't ever get there. Lack
of intention is why we feel helpless and powerless in our
finances. A financial life without clear intention is a life lived
"out of order."

Many people think it's kind of cute to be disorganized and
disorderly. That it seems spontaneous and real. But "out of order"
is the sign we hang on something that's broken down.

For me, going to college for eight years without any idea of what I wanted from college is an example of how a deficit in intention can lead to pain, confusion, and disorder. And lack of wealth. Many of my more purposeful friends went right from college into a related field that paid them well.

But I didn't know what I wanted! I couldn't decide. This purpose-deciding muscle in me was weak. It couldn't crack a walnut.

Mary is someone I knew who was the same way. No clear intention in her life. Mary was working on a vital political campaign, but she was late to so many campaign meetings that she was fired. She was let go! No more paychecks. Severe impact on her wealth.

"I really tried to be on time," she told me, while sipping coffee on her porch overlooking Seattle. "I would set my alarm the night before and plan to be to our morning kick-off meeting on time. But something always seemed to go wrong. The coffee machine wouldn't work. I would have to stop for coffee at the quick mart, and there would be this long line, and then traffic on the freeway would get bogged down. I wasn't that late, and really I was sometimes only ten minutes late, but it was upsetting to everybody, I could tell!"

"What did you want from that job?" I asked.

"What do you mean?"

"What did you want from the job?"

"You know," she said. "Just to have a fairly good job and to make enough money and all that. Maybe even to get promoted. Actually I'm not sure. Aren't you supposed to want to work?"

Mary was unclear. She was like most people who don't see that how clear they are about their *intention* dictates their behavior. Intention drives behavior. When intention is unclear, behavior is unclear. In fact, behavior can then grow disorderly and threatening to our financial well-being.

"Our first duty is not to be poor."
George Bernard Shaw

Know your destination in advance

A deficit in intention is usually the explanation for all failure in the category of wealth. If you don't know what your goal is, I am safe in predicting that you will fail to reach it. How could you reach it? You don't know what it is. If you don't know where you are going, you will have a very hard time getting there.

See your financial life as a flight somewhere. If you walk up to the ticket counter in an airport to buy a ticket, the first question will be, "Where do you want to go?"

"I don't know."

"Okay, well, how can I help you?"

"I need a ticket."

"Good. You've come to the right place. Where do you want to go?"

"I'm not sure. I think maybe I should go back east; that's what a lot of people want me to do."

"Okay. Where? New York? Boston?"

"I don't think I want to go there, either one of those places."

"Okay. Maybe you could just step aside and let the next person in line get helped?"

"You're *not* going to sell me a ticket? I can't live in the airport! I'm all packed. Just give me a ticket. To anywhere."

"Okay. Here's a ticket to Miami. That will be $421. Do you want to pay cash or credit card?"

"Not Miami. Please. Anywhere but Miami. I used to live there and my ex-spouse lives there and…"

"Get out of line!"

Most ticket attendants would call security on you if you had this little exchange at the counter. Because everyone knows that you can't go anywhere if you don't know where it is.

As far as wealth goes, know what "enough" is for you and then make it your *intention* to always have enough.

No difference? No money!

There's another secret to generating wealth that few people ever get in touch with. Wealth comes from the differences you make. Wealth flows to the difference-maker in life. If what you do makes no difference, who will pay for it?

It is very hard to understand this true source of wealth (difference-making) because everyone gets so excited about money. Most people deal with their excitement over money in one of two ways: 1) they make money too important, or 2) they don't make money important enough. They either exaggerate and overrate it, or they deny the reality of it and repress it.

That's what humans do when things get too exciting to handle.

Then, like fat cells, debt invades the system. It is a product of the instant gratification disease, the inability to defer and limit short-term pleasure in the name of long-term peace and joy. Wealth is directly connected to wisdom. Who is ultimately wise? We remember that the Buddha answered that question this way, "A wise person is one who will gladly give up a smaller pleasure to gain a greater joy." That's a great wealth formula as well.

When I was in debt I always used to hate reading this quote by Emerson because it was too true:

> "Debt, grinding debt, whose iron face the widow, the orphan and the sons of genius fear and hate; debt, which consumes so much time, which so cripples and disheartens a great spirit with cares that seem so base, is a teacher whose lessons can not be foregone, and is needed most by those who suffer from it most."

But once I really let that quotation sink in I could see that to get out of debt and make enough money I had to start making a difference, so I enlisted the help of consultant Lyndon Duke. Because I finally realized that *if you're not making any difference you're not making any money.*

Although Lyndon's lifelong research was on the linguistics of suicide, he discovered during his studies that if you can understand suicide, you can understand all human unhappiness and dysfunction. It's just a matter of degree.

Soon he became a consultant to a wide spectrum of professional people who wanted to learn his ideas. If those ideas could stop a suicide, they could also stop all the unpleasant states that fall short of that act, but that cause us pain anyway. All good things, including the flow of wealth in toward your life, seem to get sidetracked if we are not engaged in truly meaningful work. Work that gives life meaning.

"Meaning is nothing more than the difference it makes," Lyndon told me. "If it doesn't make a difference, it has no meaning. When you are on your death bed what you will be asking yourself is, what's different? What is different on this planet because I was here? If nothing is different, then you didn't make a difference. If you didn't make a difference, your life had no meaning. That's all meaning is—the difference it makes. What doesn't make a difference has no meaning."

Lyndon invited me to visit him in Oregon to learn his ideas. I told him I was anything but wealthy and he laughed. He told me his life story, and it was very similar to my own. He had overcome a very serious bottoming-out long ago and remembered lying face down on his carpet in total despair. He didn't know how to go on. Then, in the distance, he heard a sound. It was his next door neighbor mowing the lawn. And above the sound of the mower he heard singing. His neighbor was singing while he was mowing his lawn! And it hit Lyndon like a light—that's what he wanted! To have a life that simple and happy that he could mow the lawn and feel like singing.

He wanted that. That was his new desire: to be an average person enjoying life in a simple way.

Lyndon explained that he realized that one's lifelong desire doesn't have to be for anything exceptional. It can be for a very simple form of comfort and joy. It can be for the pleasure of singing while mowing the lawn. Wealth simply means having enough.

Lyndon was an extraordinary intellect who wanted to make that fact irrelevant to his happiness. He knew he had a lot of work to do to get back to being an "average person," but he was excited by the idea of trying.

You get better at whatever you repeat

As he sat in his living room telling me about his journey to happiness, he was speaking with a very excited voice. It was clear that he was now a very happy man who wanted to make a difference by sharing how he got that way.

"Happiness and a meaningful life come from making differences. But this is the most important rule to follow: Always make the differences you can make," he said, "not the differences you would prefer to make but can't. As you keep making differences your skill will automatically and effortlessly increase. Anything human beings repeat they get more skillful at. Including misery!"

When he said, "Including misery!" he let go with a huge long laugh. That was his joy—exposing human folly and showing the way to avoid it.

Lyndon's point was a powerful one. If I could simplify my life and my work into a profession in which I was making small differences throughout each day, then I could have an average day and my professional skill would get better. If you practice something enough times, it gets better and better. All by itself. Whether your practice session was exceptional or average, you get better! I never realized that. It never occurred to me that having an average day was okay. It never dawned on me that my average day, repeated enough times, would be more than enough to automatically make me better.

Like most under-achievers I was an instant gratification freak. I wanted things to happen now! Overnight! I wanted my diet to lose all the weight off of me right now. It never occurred to me that if I would just eat an average amount of food, I would be just fine. It never occurred to me!

It never occurred to me that you could get better and better, and even get wealthier along the way, if you just put in an average day.

Lyndon's philosophy was hard to hear because I had always associated average with mediocre.

"No!" he said. "That's not how I mean it. Because for you, an average day of writing is far better than any of us could do. Stop trying to hit home runs. Have average be okay. Have it be peaceful and wonderful, even."

Many home runs go out of the park when the batter stops trying to be exceptional and just makes contact. I decided to live my life differently because of Lyndon. I decided to start making contact and let the ball go wherever it went. No more swinging from the heels and getting a hernia.

After my weekend with Lyndon I flew back home to Arizona with my head full of these wonderful ideas. Already I had begun to apply them. Rather than always trying to be exceptional at everything, I was happy with simply being an average person doing what I could do to make a difference. This took all the pressure off. Because being exceptional was wearing me out and I was never satisfied. I was never exceptional enough, to begin with. And sometimes being exceptional took so much energy that I had to take time off to just crash and be depressed for awhile until I couldn't stand myself any longer and it was time to go out and try to be exceptional again.

The other problem with holding myself to the standard of being exceptional was that I often couldn't do it at all, and I got so discouraged I would do nothing. And doing nothing is less than what an average person does.

The final downside to trying to be exceptional was how it distanced me from other people. Average people are not comfortable being around exceptional people. Exceptional people by definition are isolated from others. They don't relate well. They are the exceptions.

Lyndon taught me to keep repeating my average day, so things would get better on their own. Anything repeated gets better. By small comfortable increments. None of the white-knuckled striving and jamming and forcing my way to the top of the heap. Just a happy average person having a happy average day. I was so pleased with how well this low-pressure approach was working for me I even began mystifying my friends by signing my messages, "have an average day."

I had realized that always telling myself to have a "great" day was putting a lot of pressure on. Telling myself I had to be exceptional or I wasn't worth anything was disconnecting me from the human family. Lyndon Duke had discovered how this kind of pressure led to suicide. The pressure to be exceptional. He had also discovered that when potential suicides learned to allow themselves to be average, the pressure was released and people could live again and experience the happiness of daily small improvements.

Exceptionality is the real problem

"All of society pushes exceptionality on us," Lyndon said. "Parents especially think it is their duty to urge their children to be exceptional. They don't know the harm it does."

I couldn't wait for my next meeting with Lyndon which was to be the following weekend. I flew up from Arizona to Oregon and he met me at the airport to take me to my hotel. Our studies would begin again in his living room bright and early the next morning.

As I ate breakfast in the hotel dining room that morning a very strange thing happened. A rumpled, ruddy little man in an undersized hotel uniform burst into the restaurant calling out my name. I looked up and identified myself and he said, with fear on his face, "You have an emergency phone call at the front desk!"

My heart pounded as I left with him, wondering if my children were okay. When I got to the phone, it was a nurse on the line who said she was from a hospital in Eugene. She was talking about Lyndon. "He's had a heart attack. We think he has a hole in his aorta. He had severe heart pains early this morning and we rushed him here. He has to have an emergency operation, and he's in very critical condition."

I was stunned. Lyndon had been so buoyant and full of life the evening before at the airport. I remembered how happy he was to hear about how average my previous week had been.

"How critical is critical?" I asked. "How serious is this? Can I see him?"

"No, you can't see him now. And this is very critical, there are no guarantees here. But I did want to call you because he insisted. It was one of the most unusual things I've ever seen. He not only insisted that I call you, but he also begged me to let him give his lessons to you. He wanted us to let him teach you while we were prepping him for this operation. I told him it was out of the question, but he kept insisting! I finally had to tell him once again that he'd had a potentially fatal heart attack and we were trying to save his life! First things first! And he still tried to talk me into letting you in here to be taught."

"That's just like him," I said. "He calls it difference-making."

"What?"

"He lives for the differences he can make. He's been making a big difference in my life. He wanted to continue. That's all. Please save him."

"Please what?" she said as static came on the line.

"Please save his life," I said more clearly.

"Yes," she said. "We're going to do what we can."

I walked back to the restaurant in a sad state of shock. I gathered my books and notebook and walked slowly back to my room.

Although his recovery was complicated by a stroke suffered during surgery, Lyndon surprised everyone by fighting back and working to get his life back. Soon he was out of the hospital and living with his daughter to continue his rehabilitation. The doctors were amazed that he had suffered so much and still made it through.

I was not amazed.

Difference-making at its very best

There is a little old man in my neighborhood that I see out walking every morning. He walks slowly, with a slight limp (almost as if he's had a knee or hip replacement,) and he's always cheerful when he sees people.

But if you watch him on his walk, as I do almost every morning as I get into my car, you notice something unusual. Every time he finds a morning newspaper on the sidewalk, in the street, in a driveway or on a lawn, he always picks it up and walks it up to the front porch of the home that it belongs to. He does this all morning, all along the street, with every house he passes. He picks up people's papers and puts them on the front porch for them.

I used to watch him before I met Lyndon wondering why he did that. But after Lyndon's teaching, I understood. This was difference-making on display for me. It was difference-making at its most basic. Something is always different because of this man. With every house he passes something is different than it was before.

Before he arrives, there is a paper out there someplace, in the street, on the lawn, wherever. A hassle. And after he passes, it is now conveniently located on the front porch. That's a difference.

This man is a true difference-maker. This might not be the difference he would prefer to make if he were plagued with exceptionality. If he were an exceptionality freak, he'd probably be drunk and depressed because he had not been able to make a bigger difference in people's lives. But this was the difference he was easily able to make. This elderly man was always dressed well, and

I had a feeling that he was wealthy. I had nothing to base that on. No, wait a minute. I had a lot to base that on. I based that on his commitment to making small differences. If he had done that in his work life, then he would now have wealth.

Lyndon's words come back to me every time I see this little morning man: "Focus on the differences you can make, not the differences you would prefer to but can't."

Wipe out poverty at home

"Poverty is not a disgrace," said Napoleon Hill, "but neither is it a recommendation."

Wealth is simply having enough. Poverty is having less than enough. Wealth and poverty are mastered and understood when one finally begins spending less than one takes in. If your "average day" now has achieved the wonderful state of more coming in than going out, then you can live in the moment, knowing you either have, or are on your way to having, *enough*. When that day arrives, and you and I part company, I will tell you that I hope you have an average day.

A commitment made to wealth is not materialistic or greedy, it's vital to the keeping of the other commitments. Because without the commitment, wealth won't occur, and without wealth (having enough) you will become obsessed with (your lack of) money.

Commitment Number Five

To Friends

"Dear friend, throw the wine. I'm in love with a friend of mine."
Paul McCartney

One good friend is all you need in life. With one good friend you can know the whole human community and explore the depths of enjoyment that friendship can bring. One good friend. Feel lucky if you have one.

Then, if you wish, go out and make another one. Our great American philosopher Ralph Waldo Emerson gave us the formula for this. He said, "To make a friend, be one."

Friends have great value to us, even beyond friendship. Because friendships model something very important. How I am with my friend offers a clue to how great relationships can be formed everywhere. With customers, spouses, children, co-workers, and everyone else. Friendship offers a huge clue to connecting with other people.

What is the reason I always enjoy being with my friend? Is it because he or she has all these excellent qualities and is a near-perfect human being? No! I love the imperfections my friend has, too. In fact, without the imperfections, the friendship would not come very easily. I know people who have to demonstrate how accomplished and saintly they are every time I talk to them and these people have very few friends.

It may be that there is only one quality my friend has that matters. The quality of non-judgment. My friend does not judge me.

My friend enjoys me no matter what I say or do and I know it. I look forward to being with him because of it.

If I have problems, even problems I have brought upon myself with dysfunctional behavior, my friend does not judge me for that. In fact, he enjoys hearing about it.

"What did you do?" he asks. "Oh my goodness. Come on over and let's talk. I was going to watch a soap opera but this sounds even better."

It hits me. My friend not only doesn't judge or condemn my behavior, he delights in hearing about it. I can do no wrong. Why? He is my friend.

"Only connect."
E.M. Forster

Friendship is wonderful and fun but it also offers a clue to how to navigate and sail the other relationships in my life toward greater happiness. The vital component of friendship is the nonjudgmental listening that occurs when we talk. It makes me free to talk without worry or anxiety about anything I want to talk about. I don't have to worry about how I'm coming across because after all, this is my friend here, and I don't need to. He'd see right through it anyway. And, besides, he almost delights in my dark side as much as my bright side. He is not threatened or threatening.

If I could take that same friendly spirit to the person (client, co-worker, spouse, boss, teenage daughter) I am having difficulty communicating with, things could really open up.

Maybe I want to just experiment with it. I might want to start by giving that controversial person ten minutes of absolute non-judgment. Just to see how it goes. Just to see how it feels to both sides. Then, if it relaxes things and opens things up a little, I might try half an hour next time.

I can always go back to my old way of being. However, I might want to reflect on how much of that old way is based on fear and judgment. I can return to all that paranoia and loathing any time. That's easy. I won't have to work at that or practice that. That comes "naturally" to too many of us "civilized" humans who fear each other and perceive threats to our well-being in other people's behavior.

When we are back in that (chosen) dysfunctional state, we are threatened by everyone except this one particular person. This one dear friend. The one person with whom I can "throw the wine."

Why is it unusual to like as well as love?

One client of mine I shall call Jonathan told me once that during his childhood his father was nicer to the pizza delivery boy than he was to the family members inside the house.

"He was cold and critical to us," said Jonathan. "But when the pizza boy showed up he went into a different personality—a different moodswing altogether and asked the pizza guy how his life was going and thanked him effusively and tipped him generously and sent him on his way with a heartfelt Irish blessing. We stood in wonder. What had the pizza boy done to access this side of my father that we all longed for? We all wanted to *be* that delivery person. It made us all want to get pizza routes so we could come by our house and meet our dad."

The dynamic was clear. The pizza boy was a welcome, giving, non-threatening person. The father perceived him as benign and friendly.

And so the trick might be to become that pizza delivery person to everyone you care about and work with. A giving, nonjudgmental, non-threatening presence in their lives. That kind of connection to people that you long for is easily obtained. Just find out what people want on their pizza and deliver it with a smile.

Planting the seeds of friendship and making lighthearted connections to others improves all nine of the other commitments.

My friend Steve Hardison likes to give copies of books and CDs to people he meets in his travels around the world. He calls it "planting seeds" and many amazing stories have come back from people he has planted seeds with. Steve's habit of giving reminds me of another person who saw the value of planting seeds, John Chapman.

For 49 years, John Chapman roamed the American countryside, planting apple trees. He planted apple orchards in the wildernesses of Pennsylvania, Ohio, Kentucky, Illinois and Indiana, spanning an estimated area of 100,000 square miles. Some of these trees are still bearing fruit after 150 years.

The reason for Chapman's activity is unknown, although it's said he dreamed of a land covered with blossoming apple trees; of a land where no one went hungry because apples were plentiful.

John Chapman's devotion and courage were legendary even in his own time. He walked alone in the wilderness, without a weapon of any kind. He chopped down no trees, and killed no animals. He was respected and appreciated by the native American tribes and the new settlers alike. He lived simply, and it was assumed that he "had" nothing to his name.

Yet after his death, it was discovered that Chapman was not poor at all. He owned and leased many large areas of land—on which he planted apple trees, of course.

Chapman died at the age of 70, in the home of his friend William Worth, near Fort Wayne, Indiana. He lies buried there under the epitaph "He lived for others."

The longevity of trees and their ability to spread their seeds and botanical friendship makes John Chapman's contribution perhaps the most lasting in American history. John's apple trees have endured and multiplied, changing the face and food of a continent. All from a gentle man, possessed by a strange and wonderful dream. Children today read about him and know him as "Johnny Appleseed."

Friendship can be spread the same way, planting seeds of appreciation and gratitude in all your communications. Maybe one of your kids will come to you one day complaining that they don't have any friends and you can say, like Emerson said, "To make a friend, be one."

Commitment Number Six

To Commitment

"The greater danger for most of us is not that our aim is too high
and we miss it, but that it is too low and we reach it."
Michelangelo

A commitment is simply a decision you make. And it can be internal, and voiceless and more quiet than a mouse moving across your mousepad. It can sometimes express itself like this: "I'm doing this."

As you make each of these ten commitments, you'll realize a very empowering sense of balance. Where life might have felt badly out of balance, this new feeling of balance (known as synergy) will be quite welcome. And to some of you, surprisingly so! It was to me.

Because I used to hate the whole idea of balance. The whole idea of it! I somehow knew that my failures in the past had been related to straying off the path. That I had failed because I got distracted. I never stayed with anything long enough to see it through. I was easily discouraged.

So then you talk to me about balance? I needed the opposite! I needed focus! I needed monomania. Drive and one-pointed thinking. Balance suggested too many irons in the fire. Not succeeding because I am doing too many things. Jack of all trades and master of none. And master of none meant poverty and failure.

Because wealth came (did it not?) from finding one thing, One Thing to be good at and focus on until good becomes great. The one thing you do better than anyone else does. Do what you love and the money will follow, right?

Balance, as a concept, seemed to undermine that. It seemed to threaten to spread a person like me too thin. Balance seemed like the enemy.

Rather let me obsess! Magnificently. People speak of having a magnificent obsession, they do not use the word "magnificent" to describe one's balance.

But I was blind. I was wrong. I was selling balance short. I wasn't understanding how powerful a person could be if all of one's commitments were balanced, and no one commitment was being neglected in the name of another.

Neglected like Walt Disney was said to neglect members of his family. He got so unbalanced that he actually said, with pride, during an obsessive time with his career, "I love Mickey Mouse more than any woman I've ever known."

Getting clear on what I'm committed to

The news shows on television had begun to feature stories about missing women. For some reason the subject was fascinating to people and drove the ratings up. When yet another young woman went missing in Utah, I sent a message to a friend who was celebrating how the community was pulling together in its search efforts. But I saw it differently. I saw lack of commitment. I saw the happy faces of people baking cookies and making an excellent adventure out of the search as a deep confusion about the nature of commitment. I stared at my TV and saw a big Sunday outing with laughing Stepford wives' faces and hugs and fun. I wrote to my friend that it was troublesome to me. All this celebration of cooperation. What about the missing girl? What about the person who did this to her? Where's our commitment here? All this happy camper stuff is disturbing.

My friend shot back to me: "What? You'd rather have the agencies at odds with one another and not be cooperating? Sometimes in spite of everyone volunteering, and doing their best job, things don't have happy endings. Or there isn't a resolution. Life is messy that way."

And I shot back, "No. A committed life is not messy. My point was that this show, and similar ones, are so loaded down with people congratulating each other for such really good work that we are missing the point that the poor young woman has not been found.

And I think that the attitude in this case is pervasive: everyone is so nice and wonderful and beyond question. Even the abductor was said by witnesses to be nice. This kind of sweetness tends to get in the way of a commitment to results and outcomes…it is a celebration of *trying* over a celebration of achievement. To hear these people talk, we should just close up this investigation and have a national holiday to salute this wonderful community for how hard they have worked on this wonderful nice community project. I find it all to be rather sickening, it's so excessive. Especially all these self-congratulatory litanies of exact dollar amounts spent so selflessly by so many nice people on this community project. They are treating it like a church treasure hunt instead of a crime. Memo to that nice community and that nice perpetrator: it's okay to be p**d OFF and demand answers and take names and kick some A** over this obscenity. There is nothing nice about any of this. This truly stinks."

The commitment to finding the lost woman had transformed into a happy picnic. In that, the deeper commitment was lost in the sun. The deeper commitment might have been to eliminate how okay it has become to simply take a woman and use her as a possession (or, worse, to do that and then destroy her afterward). I thought it was stronger to commit to that. Commitments are important.

"It's the Ted Bundys that get television coverage, not the thousands of self-actualizers who work away at self-transformation quietly and anonymously. And it's their influence, not that of the Ted Bundys, that will shape the face of the 21st century."
Gary Lachman

Commitment allows for backsliding

Virginia was another friend who had attended a workshop I'd given. She enjoyed some immediate breakthroughs in her work and her relationships when she took back the ownership of her life, but then she drifted back into her old victim ways.

Virginia wrote to me in panic and distress. How could this have happened? If the breakthroughs and insights were real, why would she slide back?

I tried to explain to her that people backslide. It's human and to be expected. It's even good to experience it. To find out that you are human and not changeable into superhuman. You must do your life as a human and not a superhuman. Let the backslide happen and start again. That's the cycle. And it's good, not bad.

She wrote back, "I have faced this backsliding in the past, and I have taken it as *a sign that I shouldn't continue.* But now that I know it is a normal process in improving yourself, I won't let it have such power over me."

Okay, Virginia, remember that not only is it *normal*, backsliding can become almost welcome, like the sun going down at the end of a long day. Just keep starting over and you'll soon find you're always starting over from a stronger place.

Commitment means starting over. Again and again. And then being surprised at how far you've come, again and again.

Commitment is a deep way of *being*

Commitment looks like it's about what you are *doing*. But the beauty of commitment is that it runs deeper than that. Commitment changes more than what you are doing, it ultimately changes who you are *being*.

When I was in the music business, I wrote songs with my partner, and we thought the one thing we needed (everyone in the business seemed to back this up) was a breakthrough top hit song. Finally we had a hit song on the country charts. But we were not home free at all. Because of who we were being. Not what we were *doing*. We could have had three more hits, and we'd still be, in my opinion, out of country music by now, because of who we were being. We were seeking success, but not *being* successful.

When you live for the future you lose the present moment. You miss the point that everything good happens right now. Nothing ever happens in the future. Today's disappointing status quo, when looked at deeply enough, was yesterday's imagined heaven! Many years ago, if you told me I'd be an author with hundreds of thousands of books sold and that I was a popular public speaker, I'd have fallen out of the chair, stunned at the news of such unexpected good fortune. I would have certainly said that my life had "turned out!" (Like we say of our kids, "I think he's going to turn out just fine!" when the kid's already fine and always has been.)

Yet I still catch myself thinking, "Pretty soon it will be enough. This career is going to turn out some day."

But nothing is going to "turn out" if I keep thinking about it that way. If I keep looking to the future for my deliverance, it will never "turn out" because I've trained my mind to live in the future.

Just like training the dog to use the doggy door, after awhile it can't *not* use the door. When you train your mind to live in the future, to imagine its happiness in the future, then when you get to the future the mind is already out there in the *next future* looking for its happiness *there*. You can't bring the mind back to enjoy the present moment. It's already out the door.

Anything we can imagine that would "work out" or "turn out great" will transform, over time, into a huge disappointment as long as who we are *being* is trying to find a way for life to turn out the way we think it should.

Living inside that paradigm, which might be called The Future Paradigm, guarantees a pretty equal amount of satisfaction and dissatisfaction. An absolutely equal amount of disappointment and living-up-to-expectations. No matter what you do. No matter what I do. The levels will never change! Because the mind keeps hoping things "will" turn out. Someday. Somewhere. We'll find a new way of living. We'll find a way of forgiving.

So the true practice for me is to learn to operate *outside* that paradigm…to stay in the Now…to live in the moment…to do good work…the inspiring chapter written, the involving new seminar exercise…because when I am swept up in my work, I am not inside a dysfunctional paradigm. I am operating outside all expectations and just flying.

Otherwise, who I have been *being* all my life returns so quickly to the world of other people's expectations. A toxic world, indeed.

Stop hoping that things will turn out

Stepping gracefully into a brave new world of difference-making work is the practice I now practice. Although like everyone I tend to wake up each day into the old paradigm. We wake up into the world of *what should be/what shouldn't be*, which soon becomes the world of "I hope it all turns out okay."

Did things turn out okay for James Dean, or Marlon Brando or Sylvia Plath? No. Life wasn't what it should have been, especially at the end. (Or at the beginning, especially. Or no, wait, it *really* wasn't what it should have been in the middle of their lives!!!!) It *never* turns out when you think down low on that level.

But for Dean, Brando and Plath there were moments, weren't there? Certain scenes, certain poems. We thought: wow.

Those moments were their whole lives in expression. Because life is right here right now in the moment.

And that's the beauty of making a commitment to commitment: To have all of life exist in that wow moment.

When one has trained oneself to live in the future, nothing ever turns out. It's always a damned shame, compared to how it should have been. What a shame about John Keats and John Kennedy. My father. Not as it should have been. He should have stopped drinking!

I finally realized that I cannot win this game. Nothing I could do would ever be what it really should have been. You can't even *lose* this game gracefully. It isn't a loss, it's something that never should have even happened. It's not as if you could say that the home team lost, but they played so hard and gave us so much entertainment that we loved them all the same. No. Not the game of I Hope The Future Turns Out Okay. When that sick game is over, you don't say, "I wish we hadn't lost," you say, "given what happened in that game, IT NEVER SHOULD HAVE BEEN PLAYED!"

Can you imagine driving home from the baseball game, and all of us saying, "That game never should have been played. They never should have thrown out the first pitch. They shouldn't have sung the national anthem."

Because the baseball game is so clearly a game, those words would never be spoken. You would be a candidate for the insane asylum if you said or thought that. Rightfully so.

Yet. About our lives? We *do* think that way! And that's what makes us so afraid to make mistakes, look foolish, take risks or really go for it. We take our lives and personalities seriously, and there's nothing serious about them at all. They are just opportunities to get a game going.

My wife Kathy sent me a quote today she found on a website about a woman who had lost 100 pounds. It's an interesting quote because it reflects what commitment does once it's made. The woman was talking about an inspiring insight that had hit her over the head one day.

"It's not how I feel," she said. "It's what has to be done."

That's the thought the woman used to get herself to the gym when she felt fat and intimidated. "It's not how I *feel*, it's what has to be done."

Things happen when you commit to them. That's why it is important to have a highly-conscious commitment to commitment itself. If one of these ten key elements of a successful life are out of alignment, the place to look is commitment. Lack of skill is not the problem, lack of commitment is.

The beauty is that once you learn to commit and keep that commitment you are in charge of your success. You always were in charge of it, but with commitment you know that fact experientially and it's exciting.

It's not how you feel. It's what has to be done.

Commitment Number Seven

To Your Partner

*"We waste time looking for the perfect lover,
instead of creating the perfect love."*
Tom Robbins

If you have a partner right now, stop judging and evaluating that partner. Stop critiquing and keeping score. Stop holding up judges' cards and calling out numbers. Just appreciate and let live.

"The deepest craving in human nature," said William James, "is appreciation."

Without a commitment to appreciation of your partner, the relationship goes out of control, and control is what you want. Not control of your partner, but control of how you feel about her.

As far as your relationship with your partner is concerned, you will want to make the differences you can make, and not the differences you would like to make but can't. It's the giving of appreciation you can control, not the getting. So forget about the getting. That will happen on its own. You don't need to push the river. Or, to rush in on the wave of another metaphor, if you pull up on the seat while the airplane is lifting off you don't help it lift off one bit.

Always focus on what you can do something about.

"But what if she keeps criticizing *me*?" Trent asked me one day as we were discussing how his wife was making his relationship almost impossible to enjoy.

"It's a partnership, not a judging contest," I said. "Back off and she will back off."

"She starts it."

"It doesn't matter, just back off and hook into your higher spiritual purpose, to serve and celebrate everyone you love and care for, your partner, your family, your friends and your customers, internal and external."

"What if it doesn't work?"

"It works. I've tried it."

"What if I relapse?"

I almost told Trent to "be patient." But because of what I have learned and applied from Shrunyu Suzuki, I told Trent to "be constant."

Suzuki said, in *Zen Mind, Beginner's Mind*, "The usual translation of the Japanese word *nin* is 'patience,' but perhaps 'constancy' is a better word. You must *force* yourself to be patient, but in constancy there is no particular effort involved—there is only the unchanging ability to accept things as they are."

Trent is like so many of my coaching clients who use a segment of their session for family issues, especially when those issues are getting in the way of career focus and success. Often it's about a partner. A wife, or husband, or any kind of life partner.

I am not a marriage counselor, so I simply use the same advice I give for professional relationships that are not working. It seems to get good results. It can be summed up in two words: "Stop disagreeing."

"Hate is the consequence of fear; we fear something before we hate it;
a child who fears noises becomes a man who hates noise."
Cyril Connoly

My client named Boris came to me once with a problem he was having with his reputation at work. Boris was a CEO whose employees didn't trust him. They didn't trust his requests to be open and forthright with him. It showed up on the employee surveys.

So I decided to get to the bottom of this. I followed Boris around for a few work days, sitting in meetings with him with his various teams and even in his one-on-one meetings. Pretty soon his problem with trust became clear. So I gave him an assignment.

"I'm giving you an assignment, Boris," I said.

"Well, okay, you're my coach, and I guess it's what I pay you for, so whip it on me," said Boris, "what is it?"

"Stop disagreeing with people," I said.

"What do you mean by that exactly?"

"For two weeks, I don't want you to disagree with anyone, no matter what. Not just at work, but at home, too. Your wife and kids included. No disagreeing."

Boris looked stunned. Then he looked puzzled.

"I don't know how that would be possible," he said. "What am I supposed to do. Do I just remain silent? Put duct tape over my mouth for two weeks?"

"No, not at all. Just don't disagree."

"Do I lie and pretend I agree with things I don't agree with?"

"No, no. no! Don't lie or pretend. Just don't disagree. Stop disagreeing. It's an exercise. Exercise leads to strength."

"Well," said Boris, "I'm afraid I'm confused. I don't know how this would work unless I just remained silent."

"If you want to continue to talk and interact with and support your employees and family members, then I'll give you an idea about how to do that, but you'll have to be willing to change how you listen to people."

"Don't I listen to people? Is that what you're saying?"

"Oh, you listen, but you listen from a very dysfunctional place. You listen to people from whether or not you agree with them. When someone speaks to you, the first thing you try to determine for yourself is whether or not you agree with what they are saying."

"What's wrong with that?"

"Look at your employee surveys."

"Disagreement wasn't mentioned."

"Disagreement leads to distrust. It makes you disagreeable."

"What other option do I have?"

"How about listening for something else? Instead of listening for whether you agree with them, listen instead for the value in what they are saying."

"Listen for the value?"

"Listen for the value."

"What if it has no value?"

"Who has no value? If you hire people who have no value, then we have a hiring issue, not a CEO trust issue."

"Okay, okay, I see what you mean. Even if I don't agree precisely with what they are saying, what I talk about when I talk to them is the value in what they said?"

"You've got it. There's value in every idea. Your job is to find it and comment on it," I said.

"At home, too? Does the assignment carry over to home?"

"Yes, especially at home. Don't disagree with your wife or kids either. In two weeks you can go back. It's only a two-week assignment. You can do it."

Destroying the make-wrong machine

Boris agreed to give this very odd assignment a try.

The reason I gave him this assignment was because Boris had become a major league make-wrong machine. Somehow he had gotten his own sense of personal power from making other people wrong. He always listened from a place inside himself called "I'm Right You're Wrong." That made him feel like he deserved his position as boss. He went around being right. Soon, that was all he knew how to do. But in the process he was making everyone in his life wrong, and he knew that they were very distant from him (especially at home) but he couldn't figure out why.

Boris had an interesting two weeks. Because he was faithful to the assignment.

When someone in his production meeting at work piped up and made a suggestion that his company ought to start prospecting in the outside towns where the higher-income customers were, Boris had to bite his tongue. Boris knew that the company had tried that five years ago, and it hadn't worked. The buyers in the foothills weren't a good match for their product, it turned out. But this time Boris couldn't disagree. So he commented on the value of the idea.

"I see what you're thinking." Boris said. "I understand your strategy here, the drive for bigger margins, and I like it. I admire the motivation that had you come up with that, so I have a request. I know we made an attempt to do this five years ago. Will you research the marketing archives on that and see what you think of that effort and why it failed at that time? In the next meeting we'll hear your analysis and see if you still see it as a good idea. It may be."

Boris' employee beamed.

Then, at home, Boris had many opportunities to not disagree. One time his wife Susan came to him and said, "I think we should just let Jason have his room be any way he wants it."

"His room? Totally his call?" Boris said.

"Yes," said Susan. "I think he should let it be messy if he wants. It's his room. We call it his room. Why not just have it be his room and stop criticizing him for it?"

Boris paused a moment. He realized that he disagreed with this idea, but he knew about his assignment. So he allowed himself to tune in to the value in what his wife was thinking.

"I see what you're saying," said Boris. "Your idea is that if he has his own space that he's completely responsible for, but we don't check up on him about it, he'll feel a little more respected as a person...maybe be even more willing to keep house rules outside his room...in the mutual areas?"

"Yes!" said Susan, amazed and surprised that Boris had not cut the idea down with some withering reference to the military and what he had learned in the Marines at Jason's age.

"Your idea is kind of reminding me of that old Beach Boys song I used to love so much...*In My Room*?" Boris said.

"Okay, but do you agree?"

"Do I what?"

"Do you agree that we should do it?"

"I might not agree," said Boris, "but I don't have all the answers either, and I've been wrong before about him. There were times I didn't trust him when I should have...so let's give it a try and see how it goes. What harm could it possibly do? And it might lighten things up around here a little. I don't have to be right or even wrong about this."

Would I rather be right than happy?

Susan was stunned. She couldn't remember having had one of her ideas ever considered this way by her husband. Not since courtship. She remembered that in courtship he was fascinated with her thinking, amazed at how different she was, and that he loved it.

Later, Boris told me the same thing.

"When we were courting, I loved all the differences," he said. "They made Susan exciting to me. I looked forward to how much fun it was going to be to learn the way she saw things. I even remember telling all my friends in a very excited way that we were as different as night and day. And that I loved it. It made it so interesting getting to know her."

"And now?" I asked.

"Well, I don't know what has happened to me. Now the differences are a problem. They make her seem wrong for me. In fact, I even told a marriage counselor I didn't think the marriage was going to last because we were just too different. Just too different."

"You can look at the differences any way you want to," I said. "You have absolute freedom of thought. You don't have to make the differences wrong. You can, but you don't have to."

"The music that inspires the souls of lovers exists within themselves and the private universe they occupy. They share it with each other; they do not share it with the tribe or with society. The courage to hear that music and to honor it is one of the prerequisites of romantic love."
Nathaniel Branden

Boris was typical of someone who had simply not made a full commitment. Not just a commitment to be faithful and true in the sense of romantic love, but to be faithful and true also in the sense of appreciation. It may sound crazy at first, but I know from experience that it is possible to make a commitment to myself to appreciate my partner. On a very deep and fundamental level.

And when the commitment feels like it's about to drop from your hands, like you are starting to drop the ring at the ceremony, a quick motion can catch it back up again. You catch the commitment back up by listening for the value in what your partner is thinking and saying.

Most of us look for way too much from our partner. We even look for our partner to make us happy. As songwriter Leonard Cohen wrote in one of his notebooks during his time as a Zen monk on Mount Baldy, "I set out for love, but I did not know I'd be caught in the grip of an undertow. To be swept to a shore, where the sea needs to go, with a child in my arms, and a chill in my soul, and my heart the size of a begging-bowl."

Release from the grip of the undertow

Someone once taught me that there *is* a little pill you can take (or practice you can do) that improves your relationship with your partner.

"It's called the practice of non-judgment," he said.

"Oh, well, that's impossible," I said.

"How much judging did you do when you were first in love and courting?" he said.

"That's different," I said.

"No, the whole point is that it's not different. So begin small if you're out of practice. Try it 20 minutes at a time. *For these next twenty minutes I will not judge her.* You'll really see the benefits when you can get it up to an hour. Soon you'll spend a whole day not judging in any way."

"What do I replace it with?" I asked, knowing that a habit doesn't just go away. Habits are not broken, they are replaced.

"Replace it with appreciation."

So I realized, through practice, that non-judgment was like a little pill I could take to make the trouble lift and the good times return.

My commitment to my partner is to love her. This commitment seems pretty complete in and of itself, but synergy gives us more than that. The brilliant biologist Dr. Humberto Maturano said, "Love...allowing the other to be a legitimate other...is the only emotion that expands intelligence." And in the words of Hamlet, "I eat the air, promise-crammed, when I am with you."

Commitment Number Eight

To Career

"I believe you are your work."
Rita Mae Brown

Are you getting all the career satisfaction that *you* want? If not, try this idea out: How to get what you want is to learn to want it more than you now want it.

You can clarify your intention and turn an involuntary activity into a true commitment.

This idea can be revolutionary. Because most people would rather focus on the "how to" than the "want to." That's why so many "how to" books are sold about business and career. You don't see many "want to" books being sold because people don't want to face the fact that commitment is the only thing missing.

If your career is not what you want it to be, it may be that "Intention Deficit Disorder" is the only real problem you have. You are not in need of a secret system or way. You are in need of a better connection to your true desire. And while it may be true that people always want a secret easy "way" to succeed, one should never give it to them until the "want to" is firmly in place. Otherwise the "how to" would be disappointing when they "tried it" and it didn't really "work."

If my teenage son's room is messy it would never occur to me to send him to a seminar on "How To Clean A Room." Because the "how to" is not missing here. The "want to" is missing.

The "how to" is the vehicle, but only the vehicle. The "want to" is the gas. Even a Mercedes needs gas or it will be useless. What gets you across town better, a Mercedes with no gas in it or a VW bug with a full tank? If you had to get across town which would you rather be in?

But this gas itself is often overlooked when it comes to career. The vehicle is emphasized and the gas is overlooked. You need the excitement of a "want to" to kick in for success to happen. (Ralph Waldo Emerson said, "Nothing great was ever created without enthusiasm.")

"You can have anything you want if you want it desperately enough. You must want it with an inner exuberance that erupts through the skin and joins the energy that created the world."
Sheila Graham

Stop trying to figure out *how to* do it

We humans make a common mistake: we jump to the "how to" before having a strong enough intention for the "want to." For example, I spoke too soon once with a friend of mine recently who was recently divorced. I started giving him wild advice on *how to* meet women. (Like I'm an expert.) We were talking about him taking acting classes, joining book clubs, and that sort of romantic outreach program. It was really stupid on my part and betrayed a lack of knowledge of how desire really works when it works. I had temporarily forgotten that when your "want to" is strong enough, the "how to" is not all that important.

When I "want to" do my own selling and earn my own money through persistence and hard work, then I will find lots of good ways to do it. When you "want to" to have a new life partner badly enough, it will occur. It is not that hard to meet people.

Discarding the "how to" is often a shocking piece of advice. It is shocking because it is saying that *what you have in your life is what you want in your life.*

Until I wanted (really desired) to create money for myself through my own seminar selling work, it was never going to happen, no matter what how-to method I tried. Whenever something is missing from my life I have two choices: I can be happy it's not there, or I can increase my desire for it (and it will eventually appear).

So when Deepak Chopra and Wayne Dyer teamed up to put out a CD that said "How to Get What You Really Really Really Really

Want In Life," they were sort of leading us on. Intentionally. Because we all already *have* what we really really really really want. That's their point.

So if there is a career path we want but do not have, then the place to look for it is in the deepest self. How badly do I want this? Why? What good would it really do? Do I think I deserve it? (And if my answers are opening up more and more fervor for the objective, then I am getting somewhere. If they do not, then I need to step back into space and time and start out in a more primal way. What *don't* I want in my life?)

That's why a "system" for finding success is no real help now. Because it's never the system anyway. The "system" is the great false promise of 99.999 per cent of self-help books.

Systems are fun and useful once the passion and desire are at their maximum; that's when you'll listen to a system (but probably revise it so drastically to fit your own style and unstoppable energy that it won't be recognized by anyone).

As far as success goes, the system is not what's missing. The commitment is all that's missing.

You don't have to make the right choice

Another odd thing is true about career success or any other success. Once you pick something to do as a career, you only have to be half-right! My friend Dale is a newspaper columnist and business consultant now and loves it. But his first career choice was to be a novelist and while starving trying to write a novel he took a part-time job writing a column and found that he loved it and then went into it fully.

Woody Allen chose a stand-up comedy career and he was only half right because later he spring-boarded up from his comedy success to get to the job he really wanted—making movies. It doesn't have to be exactly right, just close enough for you to enjoy it and know that your many talents will be called upon.

So the commitment, for now, is to what's right in front of you. Commit to the career you have right now, and take the momentum from how good you are at it into an even better career.

"Work is more fun than fun."
Noel Coward

Leave your manager out of the equation

Your work will be wonderful when it stops being a means to an end. When you can take it into the *now*, or the timeless flow of this pure moment. That's when work becomes a great career. And that's what commitment to career does for you.

So, master your work, just for the improved flow of it. Let your work show you the hidden link between mastery and joy. Don't keep looking over your shoulder for someone else's judgment of your work. Have your work already be great.

Many people working for companies start out by making a commitment to their career and then they get confused and turned around. They start focusing on reacting to other people. They drop their commitment and don't realize it. The other people are so intriguing and annoying. Soon the other people are what's in the way.

"I wish my manager and regional supervisor would get it!" said Erin in her despair after losing the footing she had established in her once-happy career. She wanted more praise and recognition. Her manager didn't "get" how good she was.

But really it doesn't matter all that much if Erin's manager gets it. It only matters if *Erin* gets it, because if she wants a great career and a good life for herself and her kids, it only matters if she gets it.

A fairly large percent of companies I have worked with don't get it. The management is so pressured from above to keep increasing numbers that they pass that pressure down to their own people.

So why would I wring my hands and get depressed if my own management is simply like everyone else's stressed-out management? In fact, there is *danger* in wanting them to improve and be better managers. It forces my brain to think happiness comes from other people's improved behavior when, in fact, it doesn't. Wanting change in *them* can only make *me* miserable.

(It disconnects me from my own power to commit and gives them all the power I once had.) If they have a whole meeting to celebrate me it would be "better" leadership and a good thing to do. But it wouldn't change my life for more than that passing moment because my good career path comes from within me, not from outsiders.

My career is inside me. So deep inside me that no one can touch it or influence it.

Once Erin cleansed herself of the nervous need to change her manager, she was able to turn her attention to her customer. She got out of herself and into the customer. She then put the customer's needs ahead of her own so that she could be creative. People are creative when they lose their attachment to their egotistical personal problems and take on someone else's problems.

I work with a lot of sales people and sales teams. I believe that selling is a wonderful microcosm of life. And because, as Robert Louis Stevenson said, "Everybody lives by selling something," the principles that turn sales people around from mediocre careers to great careers apply to all people. Sales is a perfect metaphor.

A sales career always gets better when the sales person stops focusing on herself or himself.

When does a sale occur?

A sale occurs when prospective customers believe your product will help them (help them, help them, help them, help them, help them…repetition being the great teacher that it is). A sale does *not* occur because the customer has become impressed with how proud you are of your own company. Most sales letters end up in the trash after the first paragraph because the letter is *crowing* about the sales person's company. Crowing does not make a human connection at the heart. Crowing does not convey loving kindness.

Every communication you have in your career is a potential seed. Every email, every letter, every voicemail, every phone conversation, every client meeting is a potential gift sown into the fertile soil of the other person's world. Most people during their careers don't see their communications as gifts. They see them as manipulations. They use their communications as a sneaky way to achieve something for themselves.

But your career advances so much faster when you hold your communications to a different standard: Do they *deliver value* to the recipient?

Because a career is made up of communication. It is created with communication. And where careers are concerned, it is communication that becomes the ultimate problem-solver.

My own career advanced very quickly when I started to see that a commitment to career was a commitment to my communications always delivering value. Instead of sending out advertisements for myself that said, "Someday, if you pay me enough, I will help you." I decided to start helping people right away. I started a monthly newsletter called MindShift that I sent out with my mailed correspondences. I started giving away books and CDs throughout the United States. I began putting things in my emails that I thought would be useful. Before each phone call I asked myself "how can I contribute to this person?" and in my sales calls I started right in *helping the person* rather than crowing about my skills and accomplishments. The immediate improvement in my own business was amazing to me.

Use your email to build your career

Many people lose time because of email. They have not found a way to deal with it creatively or to use it to make contributions and plant seeds with. Email has become a major factor in people's careers.

Sometimes people ask my help in dealing with email management, and I offer them this idea:

This should be done *only* if email shows up in your life as a problem or a drain of time and energy: (Some people are good at handling email as it comes up and then returning to the task at hand…others find it a major time-management problem.)

If email is becoming a time-consuming problem try this approach: Do not look at your email until you are ready to do an email seed-planting session. Give yourself a certain time for that session; it can be three times a day if you wish, or twice or once:

1. Set aside enough time to handle each email thoroughly.

2. When you open each email, make certain you bring it to a thorough conclusion, either a) answering creatively in a helpful appreciative way, b) filing it into a certain file or c) deleting. (Do not peek at it and just close it hoping you'll go through all your emails again later.)

3. The biggest problem with emails is when we give them the ability to interrupt our current thinking project. The best move in managing email is to take back your control of your time by setting aside a certain time for emails. I have a client who doesn't look at them until the last hour of each day, and then he uses that hour to answer them all thoroughly so that he has that satisfaction of having cleaned them all out. He also lets his key people know that that's how he works, so that if they need to get him a message more urgently than the last hour of his day, they call. But they always also know that each and every day he will check and respond to each and every email.

A great career means taking responsibility

The Arizona Diamondbacks in three short years went from winning the World Series to being the worst team in baseball. And not just the worst team in baseball, but after an 11-game losing streak at home, the worst team in the history of baseball. So the owner, Jerry Colangelo, rather than facing up to the horrific number of bad trades the team had made, simply fired the manager. He knew he had no reason to fire the manager. He had made so many bad trades that the manager, Bob Brenly, was essentially trying to win major league baseball games with a minor league team. But Colangelo was under public pressure to do something, so he fired the manager.

His explanation for the firing of Brenly was, "The bottom line is this: sometimes coaches and managers have to play with the hand dealt them. And in no way, shape or form is this change a reflection on Bob Brenly. Nor are we putting any blame on Bob Brenly for the state of affairs of our baseball team."

Then why did you fire him? Are you not taking responsibility for firing him?

In other words Colangelo might as well have been saying, "We fired him but we didn't hold him responsible; we fired him but we don't take responsibility for firing him—we fired him because of bad luck. He had some bad luck so we fired him. There was no responsibility involved in any of this for him or us, it was just baseball tradition. We fired him because it's a tradition in baseball. We don't understand the tradition, but we follow it; when someone has bad luck through no fault of their own, tradition says you put him out of work. It's throughout baseball. We can't stop it or control it. Anyone who has bad luck, tradition says you have to come down on them. The other day one of our peanut vendors slipped on the stairs and broke his hand so I went outside and had his car towed away and then I fired him. I don't know why I did except for the fact that it's baseball tradition. My wife was attending a game with me and she dropped her purse and it spilled all over so I had security remove her from the ballpark and dump her on the south side of town. It wasn't her fault, she just had some bad luck and in baseball when you see someone having a string of bad luck through no fault of their own you have to come down hard on them. In baseball, nothing I do is a reflection on me or the person I do it to. All actions we take are unrelated to responsibility. In fact I accept no responsibility for anything I say or do if the subject is baseball."

Predictably, the team was even worse after firing Brenly. Soon thereafter Colangelo himself was forced out of his role as top decision-maker. And this illustrates a dramatic principle for one's career. The key to having a successful career is making a commitment to take responsibility for what you produce. Key word: Produce. Remember the word "produce." We produce success. It does not come our way because of good luck and the breaks. Sometimes we get good breaks, but as in poker (career is like poker), it's not the cards you're dealt but what you do with them that makes you a winner. Taking responsibility for what you are producing is vital. It restores sanity and leverage and creativity to the art of fashioning a great career.

Create your own path to career success

It is said that I am a motivational speaker. I often get paid for being a "motivational speaker," and the implication is that I motivate the members of the audience to be better in their work. But when motivation really happens, it does not happen on that stimulus-response level.

Because speakers come and go, motivators come and go; in fact even training comes and goes, but what is important is what makes a lasting difference. And what really makes a difference in people is their growing ability to motivate *themselves.* If they can be motivated to put themselves on a conscious learning curve and from that learning curve keep growing in self-awareness on how to motivate themselves, how to take themselves up to that higher level of performance and not wait for some external good news, or somebody being mad at them or somebody wondering where the money is, if they will learn how to adjust it internally, then life gets to be a lot of fun. So I don't motivate them to produce, I motivate them to learn how, on their own, to create the internal motivation to produce.

There's a story I've told before about how my daughter was asked to do an assignment in school. The kids in her class were asked to write "lie poems," in which they were supposed to lie about themselves. Every student got to make stories up about themselves. And then I went on parent's day to listen to the kids read their poems. What I heard in these poems were really optimistic visions of who these kids thought they could be. It was interesting to me that the school teacher had to call this visionary work a pack of "lies." Because we all need to do that. We all need to "lie" a little to get us to the realm of the big possibility for our lives. Although it's not true right now that we are these things, unless we are willing to make it up and create it and tell that story, it will *never* be true.

As you dream about future possibility in your career commit to the biggest vision you can handle. You don't have to think of this as lying, because if your commitment is there, it won't be.

Success is getting *into* the box

Balance and synergy come from stepping very clearly out of one commitment and into another. Balance comes from having clear compartments. Because the whole problem with not achieving career goals is preoccupation. The greatest obstacle to happiness, to high performance, and to personal wealth, is preoccupation. People don't understand that.

When I do my seminars and my coaching sessions and when I work with people one-on-one, my clients, at first, don't quite understand how distractible they are, and how preoccupied they get. And how they wake up and decide, "Well, today, I'm going to pursue my goals," but five minutes into the day, they're thinking about a thousand other things. And the mind that thinks of a thousand different things in one day is not going to get anywhere.

If your mind is on the right path, it doesn't matter how fast you go. If you're on the right path, you'll get there. Commitment keeps you on the path.

The hardest thing for people in western culture to unlearn is the short attention span that's encouraged by television, entertainment, letting the kids rule the roost, and by letting the inmates run the asylum. And this inability to delay gratification is really just the inability to return the mind to the most important thing it can be thinking about in any given moment. It leads to a very confused life full of much unfinished business. The unfinished business then leads to drama. The drama leads to self-dramatization including wild stories about how other people are making us victims. This self-dramatization replaces the committed life.

As Steven Pressfield writes in his masterpiece *The War of Art*, "Sometimes entire families participate unconsciously in a culture of self-dramatization. The kids fuel the tanks, the grown-ups arm the phasers, the whole starship lurches from one spine-tingling episode to another. And the crew knows how to keep it going. If the level of drama drops below a certain threshold, someone jumps in to amp it up. Dad gets drunk, Mom gets sick, Janie shows up for church with an Oakland Raiders tattoo. It's more fun than a movie. And it works: nobody gets a damn thing done."

And, so, to get these damn things done, I need to settle down and commit. I need to breathe the spirit into me and relax and move gracefully into that committed compartment I call my career. I don't need to think out of the box. I need to get *into* the box.

Commitment Number Nine

To Body

"He lives most life who breathes most air."
Elizabeth Barret Browning

Your body is the vehicle that takes you everywhere. The body takes you in and out of all the other nine commitments.

The quality of your body affects the quality of your mind because they are not separate. In a larger sense, you think with all your cells. And you dream across the electromagnetic waves of your body's brain, itself a body part.

A few months ago it became clear to me that I knew I needed to lose weight. Why? I was obese! Technically, anyway. According to the Surgeon General, I was obese. He didn't tell me personally, but I read his guidelines. And by the guidelines for my height, I was 30 pounds overweight. This was something I had needed to do for about thirty years now! (You don't see many good animals who are obese. Not if they're out in the wild, really being good animals.)

And I also knew I needed to do something because every time I repressed the thought that I might want to do something, the universe sent me a little message.

Like the day I retired to my room after doing only half of my exercises to forget about my body and "lose myself" in a great spy novel. I was reading a book by Charles McCarry called *Old Boys*, when I came upon some unwelcome words! The author was describing the much-admired hero of these novels, Paul Christopher, who in this novel had just gone missing. "The Paul Christopher who disappeared was in his seventies but still in excellent condition—not a grey hair in his dark blond thatch, not an extra pound on his body."

And I set down the book and imagined myself in my seventies. How I would *love* that to be a description of me. *Not an extra pound on his body.* What a way to convey in a few short words the pride and discipline and wholly admirable character of your hero. Not an extra pound on his body.

So I set out to lose this weight and of course I resisted. I began blaming the whole outside world. My fat was the fault of society today. I mean, what if it was true? What if the whole world were talking me out of losing weight? What if everyone was saying, "Can I buy you lunch?" and "Ready for dinner?" and food had become a big social thing. What if the ads between innings of the baseball game I was watching were all about food and drink? What if there was a fast food joint on every corner? What if the movie theaters made all their money not on tickets but on the snacks? What if?

Then to make a commitment and set a goal and reach it, in the face of all this, especially a profound goal and reach it, would be something.

But it was important. It was one of the ten commitments I could not ignore any longer. Like the other nine, commitment to body interconnects with and affects all others. It was hard for me to admit this, but I finally got myself to see: your body affects your career, it affects your friends and partner and family (an unhealthy body scares them), it affects your spirit (it's the vehicle that your spirit expresses through!) and I could go on and on, painful as these realizations were.

"Fortune blooms in the light of life energy. If we have more life energy, then we become strong and full of vitality, and our luck changes."
Kozo Nishino

I also saw that fat and debt were similar enemies. They both reduce the energy of the individual. They both involve the inability to say no. *They also both involve a lowering of consciousness.* Nathaniel Branden describes consciousness as being like one of those house lights that you can turn and dial up or down gradually. In his favorite phrase about consciousness, "It exists on a continuum."

Here is what I see as a major problem for people with weight-loss. I believe obese, excess weight is a result of instant-gratification-syndrome. "I want to give myself pleasure wherever and whenever I want." It's the shadow side of self-control. The inside-out opposite and reverse of self-control, just as alcohol is a form (illusory, in the end) of spirit-control. Food is a form of pleasure-control.

People want to be in control of what makes them feel pleasant, however short-term that is. At least it's something. If they can't go to their movie theater seats with a huge sugary Coke and buttered popcorn and some Red Vines, then they are no longer in control. They are being controlled by some diet. That's why people don't enjoy dieting. No way I want to be controlled. I need to *eat* to drown out the pain I feel about being so *fat*.

That has to be turned around, and the brain has to be patiently and slowly re-wired.

Taking the emotion out of weight loss

My friend Michael Giudicissi is a sales manager at Heritage Home Health Care and a 41-year-old triathlete. When I finally chose an outcome goal for my weight loss, I knew I needed some process goal advice, so I turned to him. This is what he said to me:

"Jim Fixx said it best: 'The body is an unfailingly accurate calorie counter.' If you take the emotion out of weight loss and make it a simple mathematic equation it becomes much easier to digest (pun intended). So…it takes a 500 calorie deficit per day to lose one pound per week. If your weight is currently stable, it takes about 15 calories per pound of body weight to maintain your current weight. So…lose the 500 calories and you *will* lose one pound per week…without fail. How to do it? Keep eating what you like…eat what you eat now…and burn an extra 500 calories via exercise…a 200 pound man running 4 miles per day burns a little over 500 calories…simple? Or…burn 250 and cut 250 from your usual eating habits…or any combination of the above…Not needing to lose a pound a week? (I think that figure is high and difficult to maintain in the average lifestyle). Then cut 200-250 calories per day…the goal is to be a little better today than you were yesterday…no one has gained 50 pounds in two months...unless they have some strange illness. Don't give yourself less time to lose it than you did to gain it. I found success by making tiny changes in my diet...at first I gave up ice cream and substituted Italian ice...no big deal in my life...but I cut the fat and calories...then I continued to make these small changes...one at a time...over a period of time...so they were almost not noticed. When combining that with my increased exercise...the weight came off...and stayed off...and it wasn't a struggle."

The stars on my pocket calendar

I added that advice to the advice from my friend the writer Terry Hill who after successfully getting down to his own target weight said, "All I can impart is how I do it (to the extent I do it): It's straight mathematics. There is nothing magical about it. Your body burns a certain number of calories each day in just normal activities. This number varies based on your weight. 3500 calories equals one pound. According to weight charts I've seen, at 175 pounds my body burns 2700 calories. My friend Whitney's body, at 115 pounds, only burns 1800 calories (which she finds very unfair).

"So in theory if I consume 2800 calories every day, at the end of 35 days I'll gain a pound. If, on the other hand, I consume 2600 calories a day, at the end of 35 days I'll lose one pound. I look on these as the absolutes. So then, here was my system. Given the inexact nature of calorie counting, I lowered my maintenance ration to 2500. Then each day I counted calories. For every 500 calories I was under 2500, I gave myself a star. I pasted it in my pocket calendar. So, you mention a 1000 calorie day, that would be a three star day for me. If I consumed 1300 calories, I'd give myself two stars. And so on."

Terry was a believer of the wisdom that *what gets measured gets done*.

"When I marked the stars on my pocket calendar," he said. "I knew that every seven stars equaled a pound. The short term swings of two or three pounds on the scale don't really matter. It is the unerring mathematics of the star count that is the real result. Over time, you lose in pounds whatever the total is of the calories you don't eat divided by 3500. All of this is based on absolute, irrefutable fact."

It sounded so simple. But I knew it would not be easy. So I asked Terry to tell me what to be wary of, and how I might spoil it all by talking myself into failing at this.

"Where it falls apart is lack of discipline on the part of the dieter," he warned. "The things that I found that screwed me up were dinners out, traveling, entertaining clients and boredom with the detail and the routine of counting calories. Success in any discipline involves the ability to keep interested. And it's not easy. After a couple of days, one is tempted to say: okay this calorie counting is a pain, but it's not that bad, *I can do this*. But that's after only a few days. If you want to lose, say, thirty pounds, you're looking at keeping interested for about five months or 150 days. (This is based on 10-star weeks, which is generally what I aim for.) These are the basics of the system I've used off and on for over a decade now. And it always works."

It used to be that pleasure, or the illusion of being in charge of my pleasure, came from eating *whatever and whenever*. But now pleasure, if you stay with the diet or discipline long enough, past the discouragement, past the plateaus, now starts to come in different ways. It comes from beating the numbers. It's a game that actually becomes fun.

It comes from teaching yourself to have a 1500 calorie day once in awhile and still enjoy the food and still feel as if you have had "enough."

But to get there you have to be willing to play the game with yourself (or, to use harsher, more frightening language, to discipline yourself). You have to play as if you "have to" stay within the 1400, or 2000. Just for that day. Like C.S. Lewis once said, "It's amazing what you can do when you have to do it."

Commitment means putting something in the "have to" category in your mind. It means taking it out of the "interested in doing this" category or the "would like to" category and putting it square in the middle of "have to."

Then it becomes a practice. Like learning to play a very difficult piece on the guitar. If you have a concert coming up, you *have* to learn it. So you learn it.

It's the "have to" factor inside you that must be tapped in to at some point or other or else no breakthroughs. Just homeostasis, or worse. Homeostasis is that biological factor in every living system that hates change. Homeostasis tries to return you to the rut you are in. It's a good, lifesaving system normally. It's set up inside you to make sure your body temperature is regulated and all other parts of you stay regulated and functioning. It's not a bad thing, but it can turn bad when bad habits set in because it can't tell the good habits from the bad. It assumes all habits are good. That's why it's impossible, in the long run, to "cut down on" something you are addicted to. Like smoking or drinking. When you hear that someone who is addicted is "cutting down" you know it's not for long. That's what homeostasis will do to them.

I knew that if I played my weight like a game of volleyball in which we had to score three more times to win, then I would lose weight. I would keep score, math in math out. Calories in versus calories burned is what you weigh.

My friend Dr. Craig Phelps was the team physician for the Phoenix Suns, and an expert on weight loss. He once told me that of all the systems people use to lose weight, the most consistently successful was Weight Watchers. Because Weight Watchers was another version of calorie counting. What gets measured gets done. There is a connection between measurement and commitment. If you ever want to determine if someone is committed to something, find out if they measure it.

When I really started losing was when I simplified this system. If I wanted a 2000 calorie day, that meant I could eat 13 "things" that day. Spread out over the day I could really feel I'd had enough. I'd rounded certain things off that would average 150 calories each. Hard boiled egg. Large piece of toast. Certain piece of cheese. Apple. Banana. Three florets of broccoli. Small can of tuna. Container of blueberry yogurt. These were all things.

In four months I have lost 17 pounds. I have 13 to go, but I am enjoying this game now that I'm pretending I "have to" win it.

It's time to learn to feed the dragon

Now comes the second part of commitment to the body: motion. If it is going to stay functioning, I have to move it around once in awhile. So I have set up a weekly routine for body motion and body action.

Because motion guarantees oxygen and oxygen burns fat and that process gives us energy to move even more.

"This breath of life which breathes in each one of us is what one basically calls freedom. In biology it's called Life, in affectivity it's called Love, in psychology it's called Consciousness, and in theology it's called God. The difficulty is to bring these all together within everyone's understanding."
Alfred Tomatis, M.D.

I was inspired to do all of this by reading Ken Wilber's fantastic book, *One Taste*. Wilber is a hero of mine for having written so many amazing books about spirituality and psychology, and how to combine them to have a great life. In *One Taste*, he talked about how weight lifting had unexpectedly improved his writing! (How these commitments all feed each other!)

And then I'd also read about 107-year-old football coach Amos Alonzo Stagg who attributed his longevity to running and walking and forcing great quantities of oxygen into his system. The connection between health and breathing and life energy keeps getting stronger as more research is done. Nobel Prize winner Dr. Otto Warburg said that cancer has only one cause—the replacement of normal oxygen respiration by oxygen deficient respiration.

And in her inspiring book on energy and weight loss, *Jump Start Your Metabolism*, Pam Grout points out, "…people with slow metabolisms also suffer from sluggish blood flow. Like your great aunt Ethel, it can't get around like it used to. The Chinese refer to the blood as a sacred, restless red dragon that must be continually fed. Deep breathing is the button that feeds the dragon and keeps the blood moving."

And one morning in a hotel I had the TV on and it played an old black and white show from the 50's with Jack LaLanne. Coincidentally (or not) I had just heard an interview with LaLanne on a car trip. LaLanne had just turned 89 and recent newspaper photos made him look like he was in fabulous shape!

"I work out for two hours every morning, seven days a week," said LaLanne. "Even when I'm traveling. I hate it. But I love the result! That's the key, baby! The only way you can hurt your body is if you don't use it."

I taped a bunch of his half-hour TV programs from the 50s and I began working out with them. I mixed in going to the health club and walking with my CD player and my energy, far from being drained, grew stronger.

"The guy who's most impressed me is Paul C. Bragg," said Jack LaLanne. "He completely saved my life. When I was a kid, I was addicted to sugar. I was a skinny kid with pimples and boils. Used to eat ice cream by the quart. I had blinding headaches. I tried to commit suicide. And then one day, my life changed. Bragg was a nutritionist. My mother and I were a little late getting to his lecture. The place was packed, and so we started to leave. But Bragg said, 'We don't turn anybody away here. Ushers, bring two seats. Put those two up on the stage.' It was the most humiliating moment. There I was, up on stage. I was so ashamed of the way I looked; I didn't want people to see me. Little did I know they had problems, too. And Bragg said, 'It doesn't matter what your age is, what your physical condition is. If you obey nature's laws, you can be born again.' From that moment on, I completely changed my diet, began to exercise, and went on to become captain of the football team. And do you know something? Every time I get ready to lecture, I think, if I can just help one person like I was helped..."

LaLanne has helped so many people over the years it's incredible. He's especially inspiring to people over 50 who had given up on having great bodies.

"Would you get your dog up every day, give him a cup of coffee, a doughnut, and a cigarette?" he asked. "Hell, no. You'd kill the damn dog."

For a formerly sickly child to be fit and energetic at the age of 89 was inspiration enough for me. Even *being* 89 is inspiration enough for me.

"I can't afford to die," LaLanne says. "It'll wreck my image."

So at this writing I have lost 17 pounds and am on my way. If you come to one of my public events and I'm obese again you'll know I haven't been reading my own book. It won't be that the words are untrue, it will only be that I myself am not following them.

And with that let's end with this deceptively simple quotation:

"Discipline is remembering what you want."
David Campbell

Commitment Number Ten

To Your Music

"Many people die with their music still in them. Why is this so?
Too often it is because they are always getting ready to live.
Before they know it, time runs out."
Oliver Wendell Holmes

Everyone has a kind of music in them. That certain thing they love to do. Repairing cars? Dancing? Collecting baseball cards? Scrapbooking? Playing the guitar? Gardening? Fishing? Singing? Poetry? Building bird houses? It's your music. You cannot let it die. You must not sacrifice it in the name of someone else's (largely imaginary) expectations of you. You must not call it a mere hobby. It's more than that. It's your thing.

My friend and client Jeff is a very good golfer and for a long time he was worried that he was taking too much time out of his work (as a pharmaceutical sales person) to play and practice golf. Finally he was able to see that golf was his thing, and without it he would always know it was missing.

The whole point of keeping all of your commitments alive is what that practice *does* for you…and what each commitment does for the other commitments. For Jeff, as he walked into a big hospital to make a sale, if he had played golf that week it would show! On his face, in his walk, it would show. A well-rounded person comes across as being well-rounded. It helps people relax when they see you looking so complete.

And, "well-rounded" doesn't mean that you are weak. A cannonball is well-rounded.

My golfing friend Jeff was in sales, and success in sales is all about removing any feelings of fear in the transaction. Even if you don't literally "sell" for a living you sell something. You sell the value of your work throughout the day, no matter what that work might be.

A sales person who is not well-rounded and fulfilled comes across as needy. The three creepiest words in the English language: "I need you." When you need the sale, you have a hard time making the sale. When you need the person, you have a hard time charming the person. That's why stalkers are not charming. They are the opposite of charming. They end up in court. They have to have a restraining order taken out against them. We must legally restrain people who have fallen too deeply into the pit of "I need you."

Jeff walking up to the receptionist to ask to see the doctor. The golf-deprived Jeff would walk up without a cool, charming soundtrack playing in the background of his life. Something would be missing from his energy and from his peace. No music in him.

The commitment to Jeff's career is affected by the commitment to his music inside which is golf. (He could call golf his "hobby" but that sounds too frivolous. Your music runs deeper than the word "hobby" reflects.)

I want to get all my boats to float

A rising tide of keeping all your commitments lifts all boats. That's why balance is powerful, not weakening.

I used to fear that balance would weaken me by spreading me too thin. I thought I needed to obsess and be a laser of one-pointed drive. I do need to access that kind of focus, but only when I'm inside the compartmental performance of the particular commitment in play. Not always. Not all the time. I need to learn to step in and out of each compartment when appropriate.

An added benefit of honoring the music in you is that in your "retirement" (or whatever the next phase of your life is, preferably not thought of as retirement), you can bring the music forward even more. Your music can even merge with your career. Two commitments then become one. My lifelong friend Terry Hill was a multiple-award-winning advertising creative director for many years, so successful that he was able to retire at an early age.

During his business years he kept alive (although in deep background) his love of art and poetry and literature, so that when he retired he was able to bring forward this music and nurture it even more seriously. Even to the point of moving the writing part of it into the commitment level of "career."

Although he now thinks of his first portion of life as a kind of "waste" (although it wasn't, because many of his skills in copywriting and campaign-creation are now being used in his writing, which is wonderful writing now, including a mystery novel, many entertaining essays, a play and a book of literary criticism. And he's just getting started), he has made a transition that gives him an added reason to live. If he hadn't kept the music alive, this would not be happening.

Terry Hill wrote to me recently from New York. He and I were finishing writing a book together about Herman Melville's *Moby Dick*.

"I apologize," Terry said, "for my tardiness in holding up my end of co-writing this last week. I have been very busy turning sixty. And even believing that I carried it off with some grace, I am not happy about it. The Bible gives you three score and ten and I figure modern medicine should be worth another ten. So at 60 I am entering the fourth quarter and I feel I am down by two touchdowns. By this last sports metaphor I mean I feel I have wasted much of the first three quarters and will have to fight like crazy to put together a couple of TD drives. To this end—and to your discussion of obsession—I wish for *more* obsession in my life. I feel I am too balanced, too rational, too cautious, too un-headlong—and always have been. It is the obsessed that accomplish and build things; it is the rational who measure them. Still, my rational override would have to agree with you and Melville that obsession is madness. It's just that at 60 I feel I may need a little madness to get those two touchdowns. On the other hand it is in my nature *not* to be obsessed. So I wonder if I can fake it enough to hit my wide receiver with the long ball. (Just to make sure I extend this metaphor beyond the breaking point, let me tell you that if I do manage to get that second touchdown just before I turn 80, I intend to go for one on the extra point. A tie, you see, would mean that I get to go into overtime. In this game winning isn't everything; playing is everything. And...before we leave the subject, what does Calvin

Klein have to do with obsession—I mean how much sense does that name make?")

We had been writing in the book about Captain Ahab's obsession about going after this poor enormous whale, and how sick obsession usually turns out to be even if the quest seems to the obsessed person as "magnificent."

Okay, I'll buy this new quest Terry has to be more obsessed. Because, in his case, it's a healthy obsession because it's an over-correction. Like some Buddhists do, to get you to the most spiritual path, what they call the middle way, they pull you back all the way over to one side to over-correct and get you to come to the middle.

I will be in full support of Terry's scoring two touchdowns in his final quarter (I hereby pray that he has enough life until he is 80 in order to do this. As long as he never, and I mean *never* stops writing. That would be the price.)

But then, to obey the metaphor, I have suggested that Terry not try to get it all back in one play. You can't score two touchdowns with one play. The best comebacks in the history of football worked because somehow in the midst of the amazing comeback the team that came back was patient enough to play one play at a time and not try to get it all back with some insane trick play.

Losing the fear of not being good

Jack Cooper was a communications director for a non-profit school in Los Angeles when he and I began corresponding and soon he had hired me as a coach for six months. It turned out that his music was poetry, and we used those six months to elevate that dormant music into real live active poetry writing that he began to do each morning for an hour prior to work.

Unbelievably to him, his poetry began to be accepted by numerous prestigious journals and quarterlies throughout America and he rapidly became a widely-published contemporary American poet!

He wrote to me today as I was writing this chapter, "I can hardly believe the difference you have made. I think because of you I may have broken through a primal fear of not being good enough. You have shown me it's not about how good you are but about how high you aim."

"It is generally recognized that creativity requires leisure, an absence of rush, time for the mind and imagination to float and wander and roam, time for the individual to descend into the depths of his or her psyche, to be available to barely audible signals rustling for attention. Long periods of time may pass in which nothing seems to be happening. But we know that kind of space must be created if the mind is to leap out of its accustomed ruts, to part from the mechanical, the known, the familiar, the standard, and generate a leap into the new."
Nathaniel Branden

My friend Fred Knipe was a professional songwriter whose music was comedy, and later in life he elevated his music to the status of career and became a full time successful comedian and comic playwright.

So not only does your music balance and nurture whatever career you are now in, it often later will rise to the top and become your new career. If you keep your commitment to it. Commitment is everything.

So many people, people like my own father, become so monomaniacally focused on career that they leave no room for their music and when it's time to retire they feel lost and adrift without any music. My father increased his drinking to drown that part of his soul that had not been expressed. Very sad to watch.

Your music is nothing less than your soul's yearning to self-express. So it's much more than just a little diversion or hobby to keep you entertained. All ten commitments must be honored fully at all times or else the other nine will suffer. Not just one of them will suffer, all of them. Not just the one you don't keep, but the ones you do keep will also suffer. It took me many years to finally realize that. Once I did, though, my life took off.

Recommended Reading

The Breath of Life by Kozo Nishino

The War of Art by Steven Pressfield

A Woman's Self Esteem by Nathaniel Branden

Conquest of Mind by Eknath Easwaran

Practicing the Power of Now by Eckhart Tolle

The Relationship Handbook by George Pransky

One Taste by Ken Wilber

The Laughing Warriors by Dale Dauten

Jump Start Your Metabolism by Pam Grout

About the Author

Steve Chandler is the author of *The Joy of Selling* and over a dozen other international bestsellers in the personal growth field. He has coached and trained over 30 Fortune 500 companies and hundreds of small businesses. He was a visiting lecturer in the Soul-Centered Leadership graduate program at the University of Santa Monica, and lives in Arizona with his wife Kathy.

He has been called "the most exciting and entertaining motivational speaker alive today" and you can reach Steve at www.stevechandler.com and register for his exciting workshops (delivered with Sam Beckford based on their bestseller *100 Ways to Create Wealth*) at www.creatorslanding.com.

ROBERT D. REED PUBLISHERS ORDER FORM

Call in your order for fast service and quantity discounts
(541) 347-9882

OR order on-line at **www.rdrpublishers.com** *using PayPal.*
OR order by mail: Make a copy of this form; enclose payment information:
Robert D. Reed Publishers
1380 Face Rock Drive, Bandon, OR 97411

Note: Shipping is $3.50 1st book + $1 for each additional book.

Send indicated books to:

Name _____

Address_____

City _____State_____Zip_____

Phone _____Fax_____Cell _____

E-Mail _____

Payment by check /_/ or credit card /_/ *(All major credit cards are accepted.)*

Name on card _____

Card Number_____

Exp. Date _____ Last 3-Digit number on back of card _____

	Qty.
Ten Commitments to Your Success by Steve Chandler $11.95	_____
100 Ways to Create Wealth by Steve Chandler & Sam Beckford $24.95	_____
The Small Business Millionaire by Steve Chandler & Sam Beckford. $11.95	_____
The Joy of Selling by Steve Chandler. $11.95	_____
RelationShift by Steve Chandler. $14.95	_____
Two Guys Read Moby Dick by Steve Chandler & Terrence N. Hill . . . . $ 9.95	_____
Two Guys Read the Obituaries by Steve Chandler & Terrence N. Hill $14.95	_____
Customer Astonishment by Darby Checketts $14.95	_____
The Six-Figure Speaker by Cathleen Fillmore $19.95	_____
Employment BS by Geoffrey Hopper $19.95	_____
Ten Commitments for Building High Performance Teams by Tom Massey. $11.95	_____

Other book title(s) from website:

_____ $ _____

_____ $ _____